The Complete Photo Guide to

TEXTILE ART

Creative Publishing
international

Copyright © 2010 Creative Publishing international, Inc.
First published in the United States of America by
Creative Publishing international, Inc., a member of
Quayside Publishing Group
400 First Avenue North
Suite 300
Minneapolis, MN 55401
1-800-328-3895
www.creativepub.com

Printed in China
10 9 8 7 6 5 4 3

Library of Congress Cataloging-in-Publication Data

Stein, Susan, 1945-
   The complete photo guide to textile art : more than 350
large format color photos / Susan Stein.
      p. cm.
   Summary: "Techniques in step-by-step format for all kinds of
textile arts"–Provided by publisher.
   ISBN-13: 978-1-58923-505-2 (soft cover)
   ISBN-10: 1-58923-505-3 (soft cover)
   1. Textile crafts. 2. Textile crafts–Pictorial works. 3. Textile
design. I. Title.

   TT699.S692 2010
   746–dc22

2010000689

Copy Editor: Ann Wilson
Proofreader: Karen Ruth
Book Design and layout: Kim Winscher
Photography: Corean Komarec
Photography Coordinator: Joanne Wawra

Visit www.Craftside.Typepad.com for a behind-the-scenes
peek at our crafty world!

The Complete Photo Guide to
TEXTILE ART

Creative Publishing
international

CONTENTS

Introduction

Are you looking for ways to be creative and artistic without investing in lots of new equipment and expensive materials? In this book, you will find ways to use paints, dyes, embellishments, fabric-altering methods, and sewing techniques to make innovative art pieces that can be transformed into wall hangings, gifts, and garments. Using these simple and fun techniques may release your hidden inner child. Draw inspiration from your favorite colors, luscious materials, surrounding landscapes, or just from your desire to play.

Begin with a review of color theory and create permanent reminders to hang on your bulletin board. Fabric selection is always an interesting pursuit; new fibers and processes used by manufacturers provide myriad new materials possibilities. Today, time-honored fibers call for new consideration as silk fusion and felting enjoy a renaissance. Space-age fibers that melt and fuse together create possibilities never before seen. Pages detailing how to discharge dyes will teach you how to remove color from dark fabric using two different processes, which will give you multiple options for fabric choices and patterning possibilities. Image transfer allows you to add designs and photos to fabric using three different methods—burnishing from a transparency; ironing from transfer paper onto any fabric; and running specially prepared fabric through your copier or printer.

Painting fusible web with wet and dry pigments kicks off the book's painting techniques section. Colored web creates a wonderfully textured background for further embellishing. Painting on fabric opens

up endless possibilities for coloring white fabrics or altering commercial fabrics. Never again will you have to "settle" for mediocre fabric choices; you can make fabrics that are as patterned and colorful as you like. Stenciling, resists, and screen printing instructions continue to cover ways to paint on fabric. Paint sticks are a fabulous addition to the textile artist's toolbox as they allow you to stencil, do rubbings, or simply draw as if using a crayon. Foiling is an easy technique that adds a lot of glitz in a short time. Expandable paint adds phenomenal texture and works like magic.

Paper-cloth layering creates a whole new kind of textile and is great messy fun. Angelina fibers gleam and sparkle on any kind of project and also make for messy creativity. Stamping allows you to create exciting textiles boasting custom motifs. Rust dyeing creates colored cloth using a natural process, with sometimes surprising results. Altered Lutrador and heavy interfacings projects show you how to melt, paint, and explore the endless possibilities offered by a common material. Gelatin printing also teaches you to use a household product to successfully print on fabric in a hilarious and fun manner. Sun printing capitalizes on the magical property of transparent paint to print fabric with solar power, while monoprinting employs an ancient process in a serendipitous and entertaining way.
Soy wax batik replaces old batik methods, which were not environmentally friendly, and makes the dyeing process easier to boot. Dyeing and tie-dye sections

introduce you to the both simple and complex world of coloring fabric with cold water fiber-reactive dye. (Watch out! You may develop a quick addiction to the process and develop a tendency to cache gorgeous fabrics without ever cutting into them.)

Silk fusion allows you to use luscious silk fiber to make your own unique fabric. Cut-fabric weaving uses commercial fabric to create a new dynamic cloth. Chenille also employs commercial material in the creation of an exciting new surface. Quilted effects takes machine quilting a step further into the contemporary arena. Texturizing fabric turns regular fabric into heavily textured and gorgeous new cloth, while couching adds surface interest.

Bobbin work lets you use wonderful heavy threads, and openwork and machine lace techniques let you create patterns in mid-air! Thread painting adds texture and detail to motifs, while all of the appliqué methods give you limitless creative options. Needle felting, especially by machine, opens up countless choices for texturizing fabric in delicious ways, while sheer layer projects take layering in the opposite direction with see-through concoctions of fabric.

There is so much to love about textile art—the color, texture, and creating of gorgeous projects. Use these techniques as starting points and immerse yourself in the beauty of your own creativity and creations.

COLOR THEORY
AND FABRIC SELECTION

When gathering materials to begin any project, you must first decide on a color scheme and the types of fabrics, threads, or surface design supplies appropriate for the project's final use. Color theory is fun to learn but hard to retain, so here are some exercises and reminders that you can hang on the wall to help you choose colors. When selecting fabrics, buy the best you can afford. It is frustrating to put time into a project only to have it turn out mediocre-looking due to fabric or materials choices. Consult your local quilt shop or art supply store for fabric and material guidelines; store staff will be glad to make recommendations. Of course, if you ask five quilters a question, you will get five different answers, so always test your materials before starting a major project. As a former quilt shop owner, I found that it was always difficult to rescue a failing project and much easier to give advice beforehand to ensure the customer would be successful from the beginning.

Playing with Color

Color theory is interesting but sometimes hard to remember. When we practice its principles, color theory makes the most sense. However, if you remember several basic facts, you will successfully complete a project without feeling deflated by a color disaster or dull result.

Use a simple artist's color wheel to answer your color questions. The color wheel labels and isolates secondary, complementary, tertiary, and analogous color schemes in openings on the wheel. The three primary colors—red, blue, and yellow—are pure colors that cannot be achieved by mixing other colors. Actually, there are two sets of primaries; there are artist's primaries—the ones just mentioned—and printer's primaries, which are magenta, turquoise, and yellow. The artist's primaries will give you deeper, richer colors and the printer's primaries give you vibrant colors and wonderful violet and green. It might be helpful to use paint or markers to create two simple color wheels that illustrate artist's and printer's palettes—wheels that you can refer to as you work.

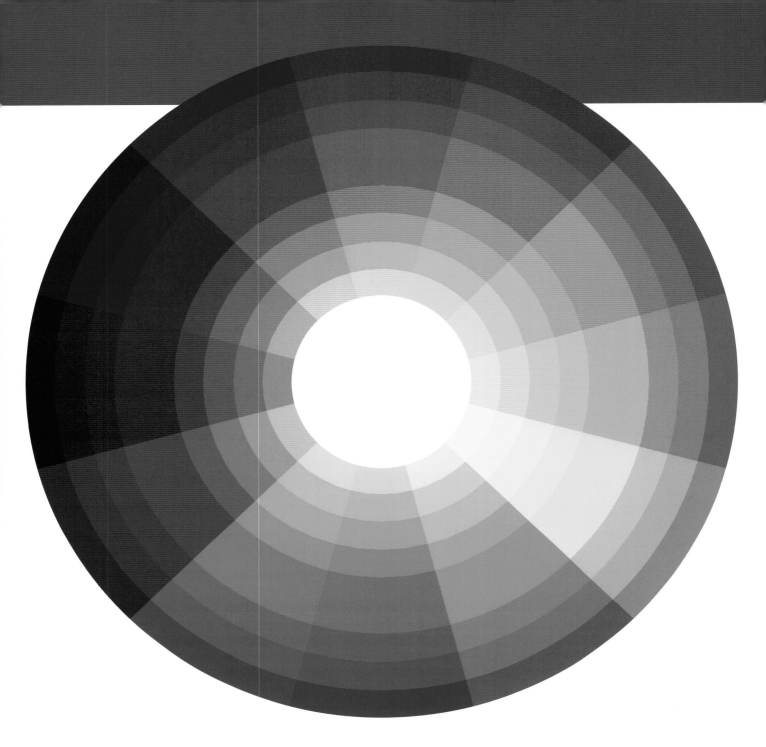

Looking at the color wheel, pick out two opposite colors, such as yellow and purple. They are complementary colors that, when used together, will give you an exciting result. Usually one is used sparingly while the other dominates. Look to the natural world, and you will find many examples of complementary color combinations—purple pansies and iris with yellow accents, red flowers or berries with green foliage, and bluebirds with orange accents.

Triadic colors are three colors equally spaced around the wheel, analogous colors are next to each other on the wheel, and monochromatic colors are different values of the same color. Each will convey a mood and can be calming or stimulating. Using different values in any color scheme will allow you to create hundreds of different combinations.

When you choose fabric for a project, line bolts of fabric up and move them around, mixing and matching, until you see all the possibilities. Need another opinion? Ask your fellow shoppers what they think of your fabric combinations. When you have selected your fabrics, carry the bolts to the window to check how their colors appear in natural light. Once you get home, you may decide to eliminate one of your new fabrics or find another one in your fabric stash—a project sometimes takes on a life of its own as you work through design problems and place elements on the design wall.

Playing with paint is an enjoyable way to absorb color theory. Seeing how some colors influence others becomes immediately apparent when you mix blue with yellow to make green. Wonderful greens and browns can be mixed with complementary colors; it is fun to see how many variations you can get by using just two opposite colors of paint, no matter which two. Try mixing white into a color to make a tint or adding black to make a shade. Try making eight values of one color with the pure color on one end of the scale.

Most importantly, you will find that working with color is fun, and that you gain confidence every time you pick out colors for a project. Challenge yourself to try colors that you don't usually use, and take inspiration from color schemes that work in the world around you. We never outgrow our yearning for that big box of crayons!

Fabric Color Wheel

YOU WILL NEED

- twelve-step bundle of hand-dyed color wheel fabrics (see resources)

- Wonder-Under fusible web

- scissors

- black felt fabric

- inkjet-pretreated fabric (see resources)

Make a traditional Dresden Plate quilt block with twelve petals to create an attractive fabric color wheel. Placing the wheel on a black background "pops" the colors. Use a button or fabric yo-yo to finish the wheel's center.

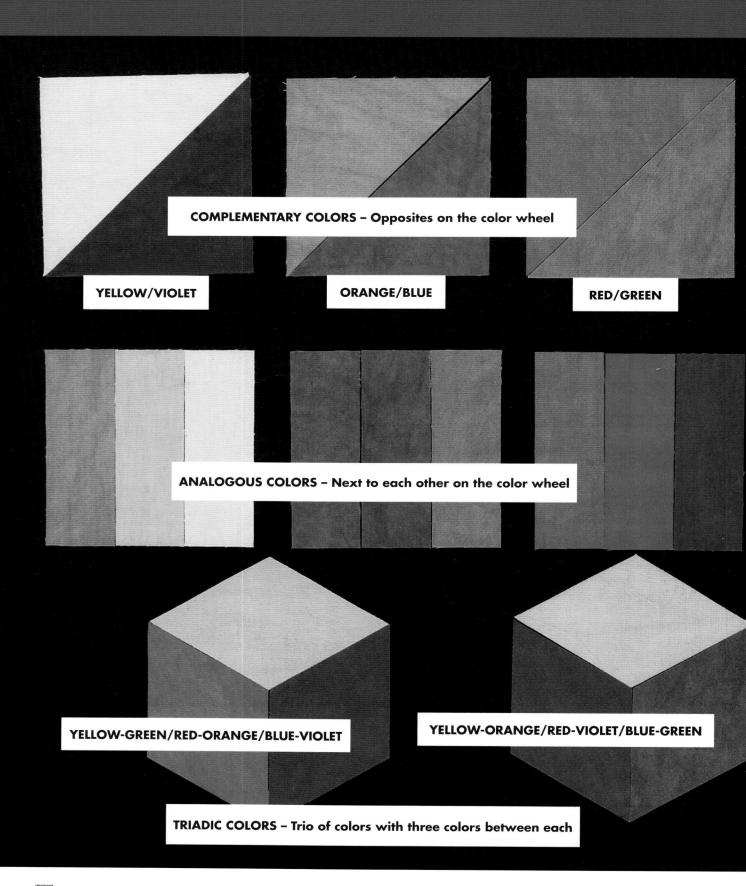

COMPLEMENTARY COLORS – Opposites on the color wheel

YELLOW/VIOLET   ORANGE/BLUE   RED/GREEN

ANALOGOUS COLORS – Next to each other on the color wheel

YELLOW-GREEN/RED-ORANGE/BLUE-VIOLET   YELLOW-ORANGE/RED-VIOLET/BLUE-GREEN

TRIADIC COLORS – Trio of colors with three colors between each

YELLOW-ORANGE/BLUE-VIOLET

YELLOW-GREEN/RED-VIOLET

ORANGE/VIOLET/GREEN

Color Theory Graphics

A fun and helpful way to learn color theory is to buy a bundle of twelve color-wheel dyed fabrics and play with possible combinations.

1 Complementary colors are easy to find on the wheel since they are opposite each other. Cut half-square triangles of different combinations and glue them together to create squares.

2 To represent analogous colors, cut three 1" x 3" (2.5 x 7.5 cm) rectangles of colors next to each other on the color wheel and make Rail Fence blocks. Apply fusible web to fabrics' backs before you cut out blocks, and then iron cutout blocks onto a piece of black felt or a sketchbook page.

3 Triadic color schemes are often beautiful and appear complex until you see how the colors fall on a color wheel, with three colors between each triadic color. Cut 60-degree diamonds out of fabrics in three colors equidistant from each other on the wheel and glue them into cubes.

4 To make labels for your swatches, type color names into your computer, insert a sheet of inkjet-pretreated fabric into the printer, and hit print. Tear the paper backing off the fabric and iron on fusible web. Cut the labels apart and iron them onto your color theory chart.

Cool versus Warm

1 To illustrate cool versus warm colors and the moods they convey, cut an 8" x 2" (20.5 x 5 cm) strip from each color wheel fusible-backed fabric. Divide the strips into two groups: cool colors (purple through yellow-green) and warm colors (yellow through red-violet).

2 Fuse the cool-color strips onto a 12" x 16" (30.5 x 40.5 cm) background fabric. Repeat for warm-color strips.

3 Cut simple tree shapes out of fusible-backed black fabric and iron on top of the colored strips.

Color Reference

If you have wall space available in your sewing room, make a color-reference bulletin board that spotlights these color exercises, as well as magazine clippings, greeting cards, swatches of fabric, and other items that illustrate your favorite color schemes or schemes you want to try in a future project.

Fabric Selection

Fabric selection is a key element to the success of any project, whether you are dyeing, painting, discharging, or transferring photos. Buy the best materials you can afford because your efforts will be reflected in the quality of the raw materials with which you started.

For dyeing and painting, choose fabrics without permanent-press or stain-resistant finishes. Prepared-for-dyeing fabrics are ready to color and come in lots of weaves. Pima cotton is good for showing detail, and sheeting is good for ease of hand-stitching. Silk is excellent for many processes and is not expensive when you purchase silks meant for dyeing. Look for smooth finishes if you want to show the detail achieved with painting and direct dyeing. Silk is a protein fiber, which is different than cellulose fiber (cotton, rayon, and linen), but will receive dyes and paints in a similar manner. You won't be able to dye synthetic fibers because dye molecules cannot react with their fibers; some blends will work but will show less intensity of color. Any fabrics not already prepared for dyeing should be washed in Synthrapol before being used. Never use fabric softeners in the washer or dryer.

Discharging using bleach can only be done with cellulose fibers; bleach will dissolve silk and wool.

Discharge paste will work on all natural fibers. Synthetic fibers may react to discharge paste, but you'll need to do a test sample to make sure.

Colored fabrics often work for painting and, of course, are necessary for discharging, but be aware of the effect of color on each process you use. Light colored fabrics work for dyeing and painting, but their colors will affect the final color unless the paint you use is opaque. White is best for predictability. Dark colors can be used for opaque and metallic paints; a black background will enhance any color. Photo transfer done in black ink is stunning on a colored background, but colored transfers should be done on white, unless a special effect is being used.

If you have a fabric with undetermined fiber content, do a burn test as shown here. Keep swatches and test results for all your new projects—being able to review your findings will save you many hours of trial and error later.

Test your fabrics by holding a small piece with a tweezers over a flame. Cotton, linen, and rayon will burn quickly, leave a soft, gray ash, and smell like burning paper.

Wool and silk will burn slowly, leave a crispy, crushable black ash, and smell like burning hair.

Synthetic fibers will burn and melt, make a hard ball, and smell of chemicals.

Labels

Label cut yardage with the fiber content and brand. For dark colors, use a bleach pen on the selvedge; for light colors, use a permanent marker. Or, use address labels on dark or light fabrics, but make sure you don't iron over them later.

SURFACE DESIGN
TECHNIQUES

This is an exciting time for people who like to play with fabric. New surface design techniques are appearing all the time and older ones are resurfacing. You no longer need a fully equipped studio to create wonderful fabrics and projects. Simplified techniques allow everyone, even kids, to have fun playing with color, texture, and pattern applied in playful and unexpected ways.

Painting on fabric is a common technique; paint is easy to apply, has few associated precautions, and requires a minimal time commitment. Photo transfer has become popular for projects that range from making family memory quilts to altering images and incorporating them into complex collages. Removing color from fabric creates gorgeous shading and variations on a surface. Even melting fabric has become an art form instead of a laundry day disaster! Try every technique, and then devise and add in your own variations.

Discharging Dye

Discharge is an effective process for removing color from dark or dyed fabrics. There are two types of discharging agents—chlorine and discharge paste. Chlorine products work on cotton, linen, and rayon (cellulose fibers), but will not work on protein fibers, such as silk or wool. When using chlorine, have a bucket of soapy water and a bucket of neutralizer close by to stop bleaching action; bleaching may damage fabric if it is not chemically stopped. Use Anti-Chlor, an inexpensive powder you mix with water, to neutralize chlorine products.

Discharge paste is used to remove color in a completely different way. It is applied, allowed to dry, and then steam-ironed to initiate color removal. It is possible to discharge with bleach and paste on the same fabric and get two different colors as a result. Play with different fabrics and different products to see what colors you get; often a black fabric will discharge to reddish brown with bleach, and to tan with discharge paste. Sometimes the result is totally unpredictable because manufacturers start with different base fabrics to produce black cloth. As with any new technique, test it on small fabric samples before starting a large project.

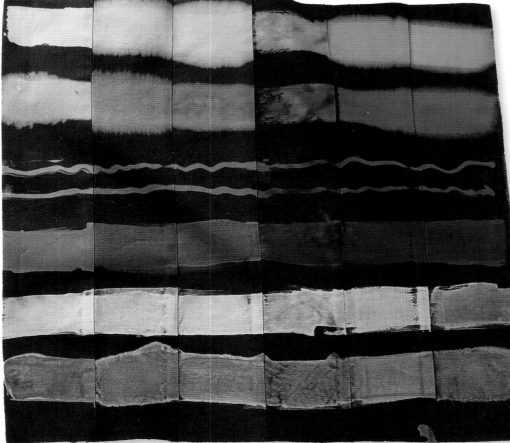

Wash all fabrics before you begin, wear rubber gloves and eye protection, and work outside. Wet chlorine products and discharge paste (when ironed) produce dangerous fumes. If you can't work outdoors, open lots of windows for ventilation or wear a respirator.

Record your results with labels that also give the source for each fabric.

Cheesecloth Resist

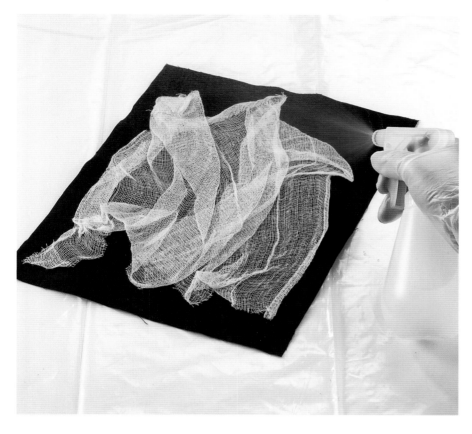

1 Fill a small spray bottle with a 50-50 solution of bleach and water. Make sure bleach is fresh. Label spray bottle clearly so it isn't mistaken for a plain water spray bottle. Mix up buckets of soap and water and Anti-Chlor and water.

2 Lay out black fabric on plastic and cover with cheesecloth or gauze, draping and doubling it around the surface. Spray fabric/cheesecloth with bleach-water and watch for the color you want to develop.

3 Once the preferred color develops, dunk the fabric into the soapy water and agitate it to remove the bleach.

4 Wring out fabric and then soak the fabric in the Anti-Chlor solution for 15 minutes. Rinse the fabric and let dry.

Cardboard Resist

1 Lay out a piece of black fabric on plastic. Tear a piece of cardboard so edge has wavy pattern. Place the cardboard on the fabric and spray the torn edge with bleach-water.

2 Move the cardboard down the fabric and spray again.

3 Repeat until the fabric is completely sprayed. Work quickly because the first sprayed area will be lightening while you continue to spray further down.

4 As soon as the last area is discharged to the desired color, wash and neutralize the fabric.

Other Resists

Make resists out of freezer paper shapes ironed to the fabric or masking tape pressed onto the fabric. Even ferns or other leaves laid on the fabric will act as resists and keep the bleach-water from reaching the fabric.

Fine Lines

1 Make fine lines or create writing on your fabric by using a bleach pen from the grocery-store laundry aisle.

2 Iron freezer paper to the back of the black fabric to keep the fabric from slipping while you write. Simply unscrew the pen cap and draw or write, squeezing steadily to release the bleach and avoid bubbles.

3 Wash and neutralize the bleached fabric immediately.

Pipe and String

1 Wrap a piece of black fabric around a PVC pipe. Wrap a string around the fabric and tape the string to the pipe ends to secure.

2 Scrunch the fabric together at one end of the pipe, twisting until the fabric is tight on the pipe.

3 Make a larger amount of 50-50 bleach-water in a plastic bucket. Dip the fabric-covered pipe into the bleach-water until the outer layer is fully discharged.

4 Cut the string and quickly dunk the fabric into soapy water and neutralizer. The layers of fabric closest to the pipe will be less affected by the bleach, which makes for an interesting graduated pattern on the fabric.

Dishwasher Gel

1 Dishwasher gel makes an excellent discharging agent. Check the label to make sure the active ingredient is chlorine. Brush gel onto a stamp with a sponge brush, being careful to get the gel only on the raised parts of the design, and stamp the design onto fabric. Or, brush the gel through a stencil placed on fabric.

2 Once fabric/design reaches the desired color, wash and neutralize the fabric.

Stitch Holes

1 Cut a piece of black fabric and a piece of plastic the same size. With a wide zigzag stitch, stitch the plastic to the top of the fabric. Needle size will affect the amount of discharging taking place.

2 Brush straight bleach (I use thickened bleach, available at the grocery store) over the stitching, making sure the bleach goes through the holes in the plastic to the fabric.

3 Turn the fabric over and watch the pattern appear.

4 Run a seam ripper through the stitching and remove the plastic. Wash and neutralize the fabric.

Nature Print

1 For a dimensional take on nature printing, use bleach-water and paint. Lay a leaf on the fabric, spray over it with bleach-water, and remove the leaf while the discharging occurs.

2 Wash, neutralize, and dry the fabric.

3 Brush textile paint on the leaf and press it onto the fabric just to the side of the discharged shape to create the impression of a shadow. (The same type of dimensional images can be created with an appliqué shape; make the resist with freezer paper cut in the shape of the appliqué. Iron the freezer paper to the fabric and spray over it.)

Discharge Paste

Discharge paste works beautifully on batik and hand-dyed fabric.

1 Make a small heavily-quilted quilt with stitching lines placed every ½" (1.3 cm) or closer. Load a sponge roller with discharge paste and roll over some parts of the quilt.

2 Let the paste dry and then iron to activate the color change. The color will remain in the recessed stitching lines but the raised areas will change.

Note: Use cotton or cotton/ polyester batting because you will need to iron the quilt to activate the discharging and synthetic batting would compress and melt.

Stencil

For a different look, use discharge paste brushed through a stencil. You will not see anything happen until you steam-iron over the dry paste—the color magically disappears. Remember to work in a well-ventilated area while you iron. Wash the fabric after ironing to remove odors.

Add Paint

Add paint to discharge paste to create a medium that removes fabric color and adds in a new color at the same time. Use the mix and a foam stamp to add pattern to a small quilt.

1 Add Jacquard Textile Color to discharge paste and test it on the fabric until you get the amount of new color you want (usually one part paint to two parts discharge paste).

2 Load a foam stamp with the discharge paste/paint mixture, stamp onto the quilt, and let dry.

3 Steam-iron to reveal an exciting new color.

Tip

Always do test samples for any discharging since different fabrics release color at unpredictable rates. Some fabrics never give up their color. You might keep a bleach pen in the car so you can purchase small amounts of fabric, test them immediately in the parking lot, and then buy more of the ones you like.

Discharging Gallery

This Trip Around the World quilt, made with Cherrywood Fabric and batik, has a mysterious "how did they do that?" look. Stripes of discharge paste were applied with a sponge roller pulled along the edge of a long acrylic ruler.

Also made with Cherrywood Fabric and batik, this Woodland Log Cabin quilt was sponge rolled in stripes, and then stencils were used with a discharge paste/paint mixture and Lumiere metallic paint to add the leaves.

Image Transfer

There are so many products available for transferring images onto fabric that you will want to put all your photos into your artwork. The products are so easy to use and require equipment that's readily available in many homes and all offices and copy centers.

With an inkjet copier or printer, you can take your own photos, transfer them to cloth, and embellish to your heart's content. Or, display a child's drawing on a tote or t-shirt that your child can show to their friends. Remember to remove the paper pile from your printer or copy machine's feed and put only one transparency, photo transfer sheet, or inkjet fabric sheet in the printer at one time.

YOU WILL NEED

- transparencies for inkjet copiers and printers (office supply stores)
- light colored fabric
- Golden matte gel medium (art supply stores)
- sponge brush
- Dye-na-Flow paint by Jacquard (see resources)
- transfer paper for inkjet (see resources)
- markers, colored pencils, pigment powder
- inkjet copier or printer
- photo to copy or digital image
- Angelina film (see resources)
- cooking parchment
- Misty Fuse adhesive web
- prepared fabric sheets for inkjet copiers or printers (see resources)
- bead and ribbon embellishments
- dimensional objects such as leaves and buttons

TRANSPARENCIES

First, let's play with transparencies. Make sure they are labeled for inkjet printers. Determine which side is the correct one to print on (usually the printable side is rough) and do a test to see which side of the paper your copier or printer prints on. Once that is determined, look for images, either color or black and white, to print, making sure you use copyright-free materials.

Gel Medium Method

1 Print your image onto the correct side of the transparency and set aside to dry.

2 Brush gel medium onto smooth white or light colored fabric, making sure to cover an area slightly larger than your image. Check to see that the surface of the fabric is fully covered but not too slippery. You will want to practice this technique before you do your final project.

3 Place the transparency, image side down, onto the wet gel medium. With a spoon or other object, burnish the ink off the transparency using circular motions, being careful not to smear the image.

4 Pull off the plastic once the ink is transferred to the medium and allow the image to dry.

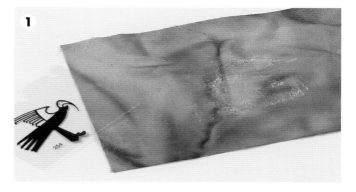

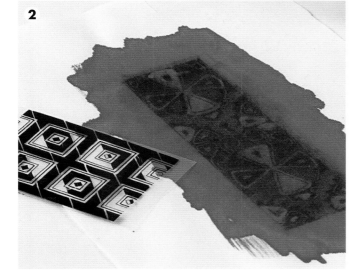

Dye-na-Flow Method

1 For an even easier way to transfer an image from a transparency, brush Dye-na-Flow paint onto a dry piece of fabric. Black and white images work well for this, since the paint will add color to your transfer.

2 Place the transparency ink side down on the wet paint, press it down with your fingers, and wait for several minutes. The ink should transfer to the fabric all by itself.

TRANSFER PAPER

Next, let's try something that's been around for a long time but has recently been improved. Transfer paper in the past yielded a rubbery image that washed and peeled away over time. Now there are products that tightly bond the image to the fabric and that can be ironed over and even bleached. These transfer papers even work on stretchy fabric without cracking. Make sure you read transfer-paper packages to determine that the product has these properties.

Markers

1 Print a photo onto transfer paper and use a marker to stencil or draw extra marks. Remember to place word stencils upside down so the text will be readable when the transfer is complete. A juicy marker or soft crayon works well; be careful not to scratch the surface of the transfer paper with your writing implement.

2 Once the marker is dry, place the transfer paper face down over white or light colored fabric and iron with a hot, dry iron.

3 Check a corner to see if the image is transferred. When it is, remove the paper to reveal your transfer.

Note: Some transfer papers are meant to be peeled off while they are still warm and some need to cool; follow instructions on the package.

What makes the new products really fun is that you can draw on the transfer paper with different media and the marks will transfer onto the fabric and be made permanent by the polymer coating on the paper.

Instead of using a photo on the transfer paper, you can simply stamp, color, and otherwise create a picture of your own and iron that onto fabric. The polymer coating will make any medium permanent on the fabric, so you no longer have to wonder if your stamp pad has permanent ink in it or if your markers will stay on. You may want to use a patterned fabric to fill in the background areas of your composition or make your art go all the way to the edges of the transfer.

Stamping

1 Stamp using an ordinary stamp pad; use markers, crayons, or metallic rub-ons to draw; or use colored pencils, again being careful not to scratch off the paper's polymer coating. You can even sprinkle powdered pigments onto the transfer paper and rub them in with your finger.

2 After the marks are dry, iron the design onto your fabric and sew or embellish the transferred design.

Place a piece of Angelina film on cooking parchment and iron on a photo transfer. Angelina film makes an iridescent version of the image, which can be adhered to fabric with Misty Fuse.

Trim Before Transferring

When using photo transfer paper, trim the paper edges up to the printed or drawn images. The polymer material that is not colored will transfer to fabric and interfere with any painting or embellishing that you will do around the edges of the artwork.

PREPARED FABRIC SHEETS

Finally, try transferring photos to fabric the very easiest way—with prepared fabric sheets that fit inkjet copiers and printers. The sheets come in various weights and fiber contents, but they are all treated to keep the inkjet ink from washing out and have removable paper backings that allow them to properly feed into the machines.

Photo Montage

1 Print a verse, poem, or other quote on sheer inkjet fabric (try ExtravOrganza by Jacquard).

2 Print a landscape or flower display on an opaque cotton inkjet fabric sheet.

3 Use Misty Fuse web to adhere the two layers together (cover sheer fabric with cooking parchment when you iron).

4 Embellish the photo montage with beads, ribbon, or more sheer layers for a very personal and creative collage.

Virtual Collage

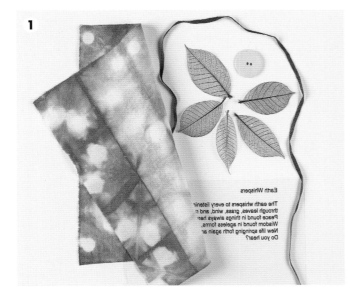

1

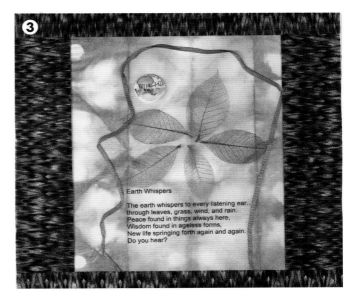

3

1 Lay transparencies, photos, leaves, buttons, and other pretty items on the glass of an inkjet copy machine. The first things you put on the glass will be in the foreground of your composition.

2 After placing all items on the glass, make a plain paper copy to check the arrangement.

3 Put a sheet of inkjet fabric into the machine and hit print. Instant collage!

This lovely piece by Elizabeth Palmer-Spilker is an altered photograph printed onto fabric and made into a small wall hanging. Using Photoshop Elements or another digital photograph program makes it easy to add visual texture, change colors, or otherwise alter any photo to make it more abstract and artistic.

Painted Fusible Web

Create a fascinating effect with painted paper-backed or stand-alone fusible web. Try any fusibles you have on hand, making sure that they aren't too stiff for the project you have in mind. After painting, the fusibles will retain their adhesive properties and can act as appliqués or backgrounds for cutouts or other embellishments.

Many different paints can be used, including acrylics, metallic fabric paints, transparent fabric paints, and dry pigments. Dilute thicker paints unless you want complete coverage of the underlying fabric. Diluted or thin transparent paints and powders allow you to use exciting high-contrast fabrics as a base and don't add too much stiffness. Use cooking parchment or a Teflon press sheet whenever pressing over any exposed fusible web.

YOU WILL NEED

- Wonder-Under fusible web
- Dye-na-Flow paint by Jacquard (see resources)
- rubber stamps
- opaque fabric paint
- sponge brushes
- ribbons, trims, and lace fabric
- Misty Fuse adhesive web
- Pearl Ex powder by Jacquard (see resources)

Shibori by Glennis Dolce, organza by Wendy Richardson.
Background is painted Misty Fuse embellished with a shibori square and Angelina, which is covered with white Misty Fuse, and topped with ironed-on organza. Shibori strip was hand stitched after the piece was sewn to rigid felt.

Painting Fusible Web

1 Cut a piece of Wonder-Under fusible web; the backing paper will crinkle when it gets wet in a lengthwise pattern so plan accordingly.

2 Select as many colors of paint as you wish (Dye-na-Flow paint works very well, along with Lumiere metallic paint diluted with water).

3 Paint the entire surface of the adhesive side of the Wonder-Under with a sponge brush; work quickly to lay down the color before the adhesive separates from the backing sheet. Let dry completely.

1 Brush opaque paint onto a rubber stamp and press the stamp to the fusible web. Let the stamped motifs dry.

2 Brush a wash of thin paint over the surface. (When you iron this piece of fusible web onto fabric, the stamped motifs will be in the foreground. You can also try screen printing or other paint techniques to create different effects.)

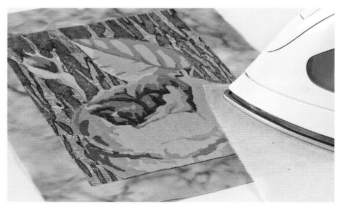

After all the papers are dry, cut a piece of fabric for a collage background. Turn the painted fusible web pieces face down on the fabric and iron thoroughly. Let the fabric cool and peel off the backing paper. (Some of the web may not transfer to the fabric; try re-ironing the backing paper again. Peel off the paper and then iron over the web again with a fresh piece of parchment placed over the web to firmly adhere the web to the fabric.)

Build interest by ironing fabric foil, leaves, printed-fabric cutouts, trims, ribbons, or lace atop and around the painted web pieces (the adhesive properties of the Wonder-Under will remain intact). Place a press sheet over the top before ironing. Here, purple Wonder-Under was fused to white before being added to the background to block a shadow through of the underlying fabric.

Cut several small pieces of fabric to test the effect of the stamped and painted Wonder-Under when it is applied to different base fabrics.

Cut shapes out of the painted Wonder-Under and iron to a background fabric. These can be foiled, outlined with stitches, or embellished if you wish.

Create a Misty Fuse Collage

Misty Fuse is a fairly new product that is extremely sheer and lightweight compared to other fusible webs. It is not sticky and can remain exposed even if not painted, so it's a good choice for using with organza and lace. It comes in black and white, so you will want to try coloring on both to see the results.

Use pieces of Misty Fuse colored with dry pigments to embellish a piece of fabric. Put a piece of Misty Fuse into a zipper bag with some dry pigments, such as Pearl Ex, and shake to color it. Place cooking parchment atop the fusible web piece and iron it onto the fabric.

Or, paint Misty Fuse and use it as a collage background. Add fabric cutouts, lace, ribbon, silk flowers, or candy wrappers. If you like, add a layer of tulle or organza to the top, which will adhere to the areas where there are no embellishments. Leave the collage as is or stitch around the underlying elements.

Use wet paints on Misty Fuse, as you would on Wonder-Under. Pour paint into a cup and dip the web or pour paint over it and scrunch it. Dry the web and iron it onto fabric, with cooking parchment placed over the top.

Plan Ahead

Paint extra web to keep on hand when you don't have time to wait for paint to dry. It makes such an interesting and mysterious substrate.

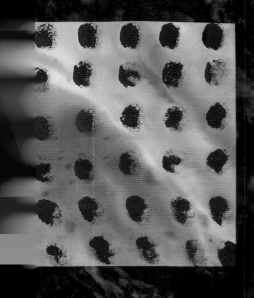
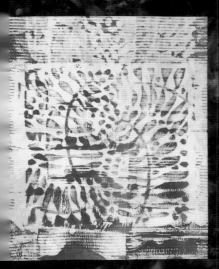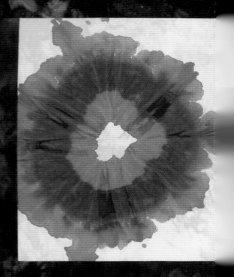
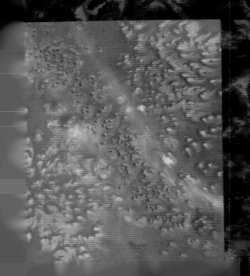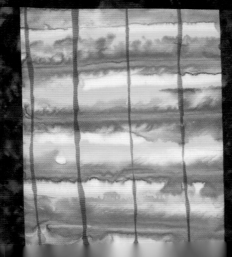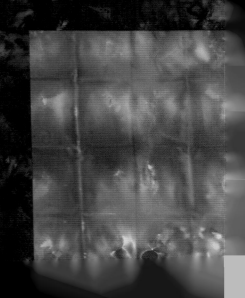

Painting on Fabric

Fabric paints make altering and decorating fabric very quick and easy. Fabric paints give much the same results of dyes but without the time, formulas, chemicals, and unpredictability associated with dyeing. The hand of the fabric may change with paints, as they are bonded to the fabric with adhesives, rather than reacting directly with the fibers like dye will. There are many brands and types of fabric paints, so ask friends about their favorites and test any you might be considering for a project.

Generally, there are four kinds of paint. One is a very thin, transparent paint, which looks very much like dye when it is applied. It can be used for color washes and effects where bleeding and blending are desired. Dye-na-Flow is the kind used in the samples here. A second type of paint is slightly thicker but still transparent so it is more controllable and can be used for stamping, screen printing, and coloring black and white print fabrics. Textile Color and Setacolor are good brands to try. Both these paints and Dye-na-Flow work for sun-printing, but none can be used on dark fabric. Opaque paints cover what is underneath and can be used for stamping, screen printing, resist techniques, and on dark fabrics. Neopaque is an excellent choice. Metallic paints are lustrous and beautiful on dark fabrics, as well as light ones, and cover what is underneath. Lumiere, a metallic paint, comes in lots of great colors. Be sure to thoroughly mix metallic colors before using.

YOU WILL NEED

- heavy duty aluminum foil
- PFD (prepared-for-dyeing) or other light-colored fabrics
- Dye-na-Flow paint by Jacquard (see resources)
- sponge brush
- bubble wrap
- coarse salt
- non-hardening sponge
- Neopaque and Lumiere paints by Jacquard (see resources)
- rubber brayer
- leaves
- plastic-lace or bamboo placemats, lengths of strings, rubber bands or other dimensional objects
- flat-bottomed containers

If you are sponging or stamping with opaque paints, you can let them dry and wash over them with thin transparent paint. Or, if you do a wash with thin paint and let that dry, you can stamp or print on top with opaque paint. After all paints dry, heat set with an iron following manufacturer's directions. An alternative to ironing is placing the fabric in the clothes dryer on high for 30 minutes or simply allowing the paint to cure for two weeks before washing. After setting, the paint is washable, dry cleanable, and permanent. Wash all fabrics before painting to remove sizing, unless you are using prepared-for-dyeing fabrics. Paints will work on all fibers, since the color bonds to the surface rather than reacting with the fibers. You might even want to paint over some "ugly" fabric from your stash.

There are many ways to apply paint, and it is fun to try the "what if" approach to painting. Equipment requirements are minimal—sponge brushes, sponges, bubble wrap, aluminum foil, paper towels, a plastic table cover, spray bottle, plastic cups, and an apron will get you through many hours of play. Remember that paints will pattern themselves on the fabric even if you don't intentionally manipulate the process—wrinkled plastic under the fabric will add lines, wayward threads will absorb paint, ironing a piece dry on parchment paper will create a ribbed pattern, an air bubble under the fabric will make itself known when the fabric is dry.

Aluminum Foil

Soft stripes can be made by placing accordion-pleated heavy duty aluminum foil beneath the fabric.

1 Accordion-pleat a piece of aluminum foil. Set foil on protected work surface and top with a piece of fabric.

2 Spray the fabric with water. Use a sponge brush or pipette to apply one color of thin paint to the peaks and another color in the valleys. Color blending will occur as paint migrates and bleeds. (Here is where you get to "watch the paint dry.")

Bubble Wrap

Bubble wrap provides a cheap and wonderful pattern-making device when used with thin paint.

1 Lay bubble wrap on a protected work surface.

2 Place a piece of damp fabric over the bubble wrap and dab paint on fabric with a sponge brush. Use plenty of paint. When you see a pattern you like, dry the fabric with a hair dryer while it is still on the bubble wrap to preserve that amount of patterning.

3 Place the completed bubble wrap/fabric in a location where it will dry fairly fast.

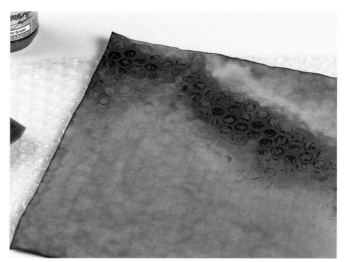

Salt

Coarse salt of any kind will make fantastic designs on wet painted fabric, and works best on smooth-surfaced fabrics, such as pima cotton, sateen, or habotai silk.

1 Set fabric on protected work surfaces. Spray the fabric with water.

2 Paint fabric with two or three colors of thin paint.

3 Sprinkle salt over the wet surface and leave the fabric to dry (the hard part). This pattern-making process will take at least 15 to 30 minutes to start working.

4 When the fabric is completely dry, simply brush the salt away.

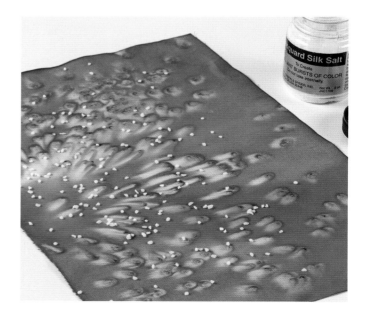

Sponges

Use a non-hardening sponge, like a cosmetic or sea sponge, to apply opaque or metallic paint to a light colored fabric. Sherrill Kahn taught me this fun method, which makes a great background for other embellishments.

1 Protect work surface with plastic. Load a sponge by dipping it into the paint and then tapping it on the plastic table cover to force paint into the sponge pores.

2 Place fabric on clean work area. Dab the sponge onto the fabric until the sponge begins to dry; reload the sponge with paint and continue.

3 Add another layer of interest. Use as many paint colors as you like and vary the sizes of your sponges. Use smaller sponges to make additional marks on top of the first sponged-on patterns.

4 Let the fabric dry.

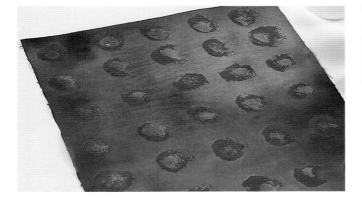

Wash over the sponged circles with thin paint by spraying the fabric with water and then brushing paint around the first marks. The paint will flow into the spaces left between the circles. After the paint is totally dry, iron from the back of the fabric with a hot iron to set the paints.

Use the bubble wrap differently by printing with it rather than letting the paint flow around the bubbles. With a sponge brush and opaque or metallic paint, cover the raised air pockets with paint. Lay a piece of fabric, either light or dark, over the bubble wrap and press with your hands. Let dry and heat set.

Leaves

Nature printing is fun to do any time of year, but if you have a few leaves pressed in an old phone book, you can bring a bit of spring into play during the long months of winter. (Of course, if you don't have any pressed leaves available, you can always rob a house plant of a few leaves!) A brayer, which looks like a miniature paint roller, is a great tool to use for getting a good print of leaves.

1 Lay out fabric on a protected work surface.

2 Use a sponge brush to coat the back of a leaf with Textile Color, Neopaque, or Lumiere paints.

3 Turn the leaf paint side down on the fabric, cover with a paper towel to catch any paint that got onto the front side of the leaf, and roll over the paper towel with the brayer. If the leaf is still in good shape, use it again for another print.

4 Remove the paper towel and leaf. Let the paint dry.

Textured Items

1 Place a plastic lace or bamboo placemat, leaves, cheese-cloth, rubbing plates, string, or rubber bands on a plastic-covered table.

2 Place a piece of fabric over items.

3 Pour thick paint on the plastic-covered table or a piece of plastic or glass. Roll the brayer in one direction through the paint until the brayer is evenly and sparingly covered.

4 Roll the brayer over the fabric—the brayer will paint the impressions of the things you have placed underneath the fabric. (In the pictured sample, two colors of paint were used at the same time. After the brayer rolled over the rubbing plate, it painted a ghost image at the top of the fabric.)

Dip Dye

Dip dying fabric in multiple colors gives you wonderful surprises since you have no control over where the paint will bleed. Color theory definitely comes into play with this technique because the colors will mix. Which color you start with will make a huge difference in the end result. Do at least two samples so you can compare them.

1 Accordion-fold a piece of fabric in one direction and then accordion-fold it again in the other direction.

2 Pour different colors of thin paint into small, flat bottom containers. Dip each side of the folded fabric in one of the paints until the paint starts to wick up. Stop dipping when most of the outside layers are colored.

3 Carefully unfold the fabric and spread it on plastic to dry.

Tie-Dye

Tie-dyed fabric has been around for decades but the technique is even simpler when you use paint to make a small tie-dye-style project or quilt block.

1 Grab the center of the fabric and tightly rubber band the first inch or so. Move down an inch and wind another rubber band tightly around the fabric. Continue to add bands at intervals of your choice.

2 With pipettes, saturate each section with a different color of paint, using enough paint to reach the inner layers.

3 Let the paint sit on the fabric for a few minutes before removing the bands. Let the fabric dry.

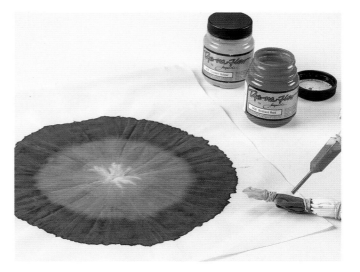

Pad Your Surface

For many kinds of painting on fabric, such as screen printing, stamping, and nature printing, place a padded surface under the fabric. Cut a piece of rubber carpet padding or terry cloth the size of your table and cover with plastic.

Stenciling

Stenciling is a great way to decorate a piece of fabric using dye, fabric paint, paint sticks, crayons, discharge paste, chlorine dishwasher detergent (to remove color), markers, or other products. There are many types of stencils. Plastic stencils last forever if properly cared for. You can sometimes find them in unlikely places; you'll find home-decorating stencils in the paint departments at home improvement stores, and lettering stencils in office supply stores.

To stencil with dye, you need to thicken it; the other products listed are ready to be used for stenciling. Choose a fabric with a smooth surface so the stencil details will show. Spray the back of the stencil with adhesive spray or use masking tape to hold the stencil in place. Place an easy-to-clean non-slip rubber mat under the fabric to hold the fabric securely while you work.

Clean the stencil immediately after use and work carefully so you don't bend the stencil's small points or tear the plastic. Blot the stencil with paper towels between uses so you don't transfer paint where you don't want it. Use tape to mask off parts of the stencil that you will be painting with another color.

YOU WILL NEED

- stencil
- stencil adhesive
- masking tape
- non-slip rubber mat
- color medium
- foam brush, foam roller, dauber, or other applicator
- template plastic, Mylar, or freezer paper and craft knife for making stencils
- masking tape

FABRIC STENCILING TECHNIQUES

For a stencil with fine detail, use a small sponge brush or dauber to apply dye, paint, or discharge paste. For stencils with larger openings, use a foam roller. The brush or roller should be sparingly loaded with medium—if there is too much paint or dye it will run under the edge of the stencil opening and ruin the image. Use a short brush stroke or dab the medium into the openings. Lift the stencil very carefully off the fabric so you don't smear the image.

To add texture to the image, use a sea sponge or scrunched paper towel to apply a wet medium. Load the sponge from a puddle of medium and then tamp it on a paper towel or the plastic table cover to push the medium into the sponge pores.

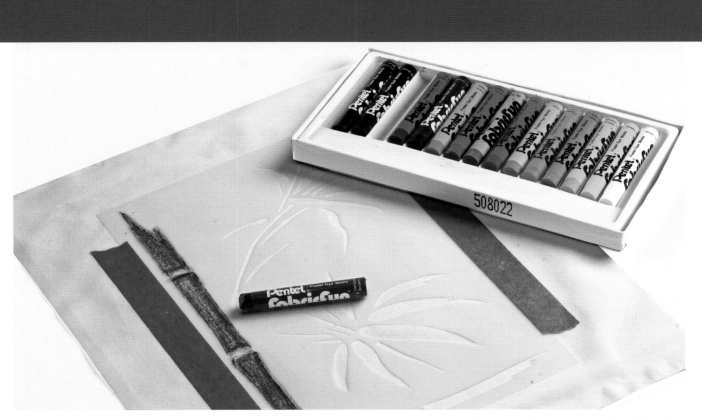

Work directly with drier mediums, such as paint sticks, crayons, or markers. Fill in stencil openings with solid color or by shading from the edges into the centers. For best control when working with paint sticks, use a stencil brush. See page 64 for more directions.

Create depth by stenciling a second time over fabric that has been allowed to dry. Create a shadow effect by stenciling the same image twice, with the second one placed slightly off to one side. With fabric paint, heat setting is only necessary after all the painting is completed. With paint sticks, you will have to wait a day before applying more images to avoid smearing.

Custom Stencils

Create stencils that you can use over and over again. Trace or draw simple motifs or complex images onto template plastic or Mylar. Cut out the openings with a craft knife.

1 Make a temporary stencil using freezer paper. Draw or trace an image on the paper, remembering to keep bridges between shapes so the stencil doesn't fall apart.

2 Use a craft knife to cut out the openings.

3 Iron the shiny side of the freezer-paper stencil to the fabric and color in the spaces with any of the products mentioned on page 51. You may be able to reuse the stencil a few times if it isn't too fragile.

2

Use masking tape to mask off stripes on a piece of fabric and then stencil an image over the tape. The image will be interrupted by the tape. If you're using paint, immediately and carefully remove the tape, without smearing the medium, to prevent paint from sealing tape edges to the fabric.

Flip It

Stencils are great for creating mirror images—just use the back side!

Resists

These fabrics have been purchased from artists who have perfected the art of resist. Potato dextrin resist with dye, folded and bleached, painting over folded fabric, and clouds made with tufts of batting as a resist create textiles that invite the buyer to create and embellish—or in many cases, just caress the fabric.

Resists do as their name implies—they resist whatever you apply over them. There are two kinds of resists, both of which are easy to use and take no special equipment to apply. Mechanical resists block off fabric with freezer paper, tape, clothespins, or rubber bands or by folding, clamping, or simply setting an object atop fabric. The paint, dye, or discharge agent is then applied by spraying, brushing, or sponging.

Chemical resists require more time because the resist must be completely dry before you apply color. With chemical resists, you have a lot of control and can create complex designs because you are able to apply color in particular areas while avoiding others. Some chemical resists are water-based gutta, either clear or colored; crayon and paint sticks; Elmer's School Glue, which washes out after the color is applied; potato flakes or powder, which dry on the fabric and crack so the dye or bleach runs in and makes crack patterns; and metallic paint. Other resists are available at art supply stores, but make sure they can be removed with water unless you're willing to work with solvents.

YOU WILL NEED

- Dye-na-Flow paint by Jacquard (see resources)

- bleach

- spray bottle

- resists like leaves, plastic lace, and cheesecloth

- freezer paper or stickers

- Neopaque or Lumiere paints by Jacquard (see resources)

- masking tape

- sponge brush

- sea sponge

- Elmer's Washable School Glue

- wax crayons or Shiva Paintstiks (see resources)

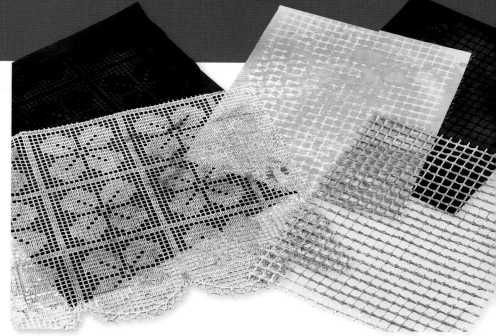

For the simplest resist, lay an object on a piece of fabric and spray over it with thin paint or 50% bleach/50% water. Plastic lace, rug grippers, cheesecloth, pressed leaves, and other things that lie flat are the best options. After you spray over the resist with paint, turn the resist over and print the fabric with the paint left on the top of the resist. See the discharge chapter for further instructions on how to process the bleached fabric.

Cut shapes from freezer paper or use precut stickers to cover a piece of fabric and then use thicker paint, such as Neopaque or metallic Lumiere, to paint all the uncovered spaces.

Tape

Use pieces of tape to make designs on fabric. The only places that keep their original color will be those that you covered with tape.

1 Lay out your fabric on a plastic-covered tabletop.

2 Cut pieces of tape extra long so pieces can be taped down to the plastic on the table for ease of painting. Arrange tape pieces on fabric and smooth in place.

3 Use a sponge brush to paint uncovered areas with thicker paint, discharge agent, or thickened dye. Apply paint with a sea sponge for a softer look. (Do not use sea sponges to apply bleach because bleach will destroy the sponge.)

4 Remove tape immediately after painting.

Gutta and Glue

Water-based gutta and school glue can be applied directly to fabric using the bottle's or tube's nozzle. Before tackling a project, practice applying smooth lines to scrap fabric.

1 Lay fabric on protected work surface. Apply gutta or glue in freeform patterns, pushing the resist through the fabric. Allow medium and fabric to dry thoroughly.

2 Use a foam brush to apply thin paint over the whole piece of fabric. Let the paint dry.

3 Heat set paint with a hot iron.

4 Soak fabric in warm water to remove resist. Rub the softened resist off the fabric with your fingers; feel for slippery areas to make sure all the resist has been removed.

Try This

Start with batik or hand-dyed fabric instead of white fabric for a more unified and complex final result.

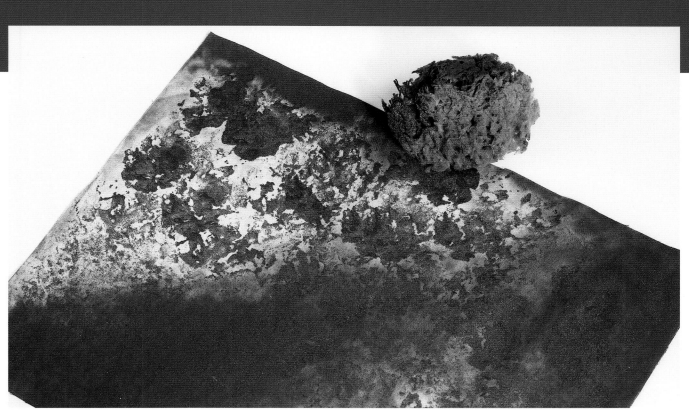

Paint fabric with Lumiere or other metallic paint using a sponge or other application method. Let dry thoroughly and then brush fabric with a thin paint like Dye-na-Flow and spray with water. The thin paint will color the fabric around the metallic paint. This sample was dried on bubble wrap to add extra interest.

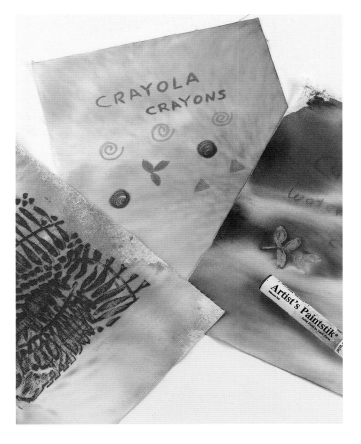

Crayons and Paint Sticks

Create interesting patterns by drawing on fabric with wax crayons or paint sticks (see chapter on paint sticks for more information). The oil and wax acts as a resist to water-based mediums. In these samples, the wax crayons made a good resist while Caran d'Ache watercolor crayons bled when the fabric was dampened and painted—but is that a bad thing?

1 Place a non-slip rubber sheet under the fabric to make it easier to draw on the fabric.

2 Pushing heavily on a crayon or paint stick, draw motifs on fabric.

3 Use a foam brush to apply paint to fabric. Remember that paint sticks will smear for two days after being applied so paint over it carefully—spraying paint works very well with paint sticks.

4 Let the fabric sit for a few days and then heat set the paint stick, crayon, and paint with a hot iron. Use press cloths or cooking parchment to protect the iron and ironing surface.

Paint Sticks

Paint sticks, consisting of linseed oil and pigment, have been used for many years by artists. The sticks have become popular with fiber artists, quilters, and other crafters because the sticks are easy to use, clean up with household citrus cleaner, last for a long time, and are always ready to be used to embellish a project. Very little application equipment is needed, and when heat set, paint-stick colored images are permanent and washable.

Look for sets of mini sticks, single large sticks, sets of six or twelve large sticks, and rubbing plates, stencils, and brushes. The paint sticks come in lots of matte colors and in wonderfully iridescent colors that contribute a subtle sheen. There are blender sticks for making gradations and lightening colors. Paint sticks work on all fabric fibers; the iridescent paint sticks look beautiful on dark colors.

YOU WILL NEED

- Shiva Paintstiks, matte or iridescent (see resources)
- fabrics
- rubbing plates or other textured items
- wire
- embossed wallpaper
- masking tape
- non-slip rubber sheeting
- letters, cardboard stickers, or Grungeboard
- stencil
- freezer paper
- craft knife
- heavy paper or cardboard scrap

This wall hanging was designed by Nancy Kazlauckas and the pattern is distributed by Cedar Canyon Textiles. The stencils for the smaller coneflowers are included in the pattern.

Paint Stick Basics

Paint sticks can be used directly on the fabric like a crayon, but there are a few tricks for using them effectively.

1 Remove the protective skin on the outside of sticks by peeling skins off with a paper towel and your fingernail or a small paring knife. When the stick glides easily over a piece of paper, it is ready to use.

2 Do not drop paint stick shavings on your clothing or the floor as they will stain.

3 Place a non-slip rubber mat under the fabric to keep it from slipping and practice writing your name or other words.

4 Set the fabric aside for two or three days to dry. Iron it on the reverse side to set the paint; protect your ironing surface with parchment or a press cloth.

Rubbings

Transfer patterns to fabric by rubbing the paint stick over dimensional objects.

1 Place a rubbing plate, textured placemat, plastic lace, or other textured item on the non-slip mat.

2 Tape a piece of fabric over the item and press the fabric into the item's depressions to define the edges.

3 Rub the flat end of a paint stick or the side of a stick removed from the cardboard sleeve over fabric, picking up the pattern of the item beneath. Hold your hand on the edge of the fabric and rub away from your hand for less slippage. For more stability, spray the rubbing plate or other item with temporary adhesive.

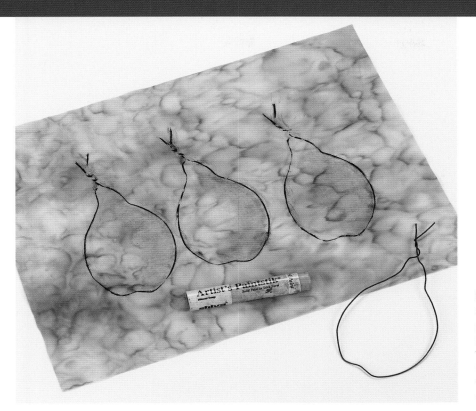

Bend wire into an interesting shape and place it under fabric placed on a non-slip surface. Use paintstik to make a rubbing of the wire shape. Move the fabric and repeat rubbing with another color or make black outlines and fill in the shapes with color.

Wallpaper

Create a unique border on a quilt using embossed wallpaper borders. (Or to add interest to an already finished quilt that needs a punch, stencil a paint stick design onto a plain border.)

1 Cut the fabric borders for your quilt a little larger than their finished size and the wallpaper border to leave room for taping.

2 Set fabric atop wallpaper border and tape both pieces down.

3 Rub the flat end of a paint stick or the side of a stick removed from the cardboard sleeve over fabric, picking up the raised wallpaper pattern beneath.

4 Let design dry and heat set.

Letters

Make a rubbing to create your own studio name placard or a sign for a child's bedroom.

1 Make a personalized rubbing plate with self-adhesive letters or grunge board letters.

2 Arrange and adhere the letters onto a piece of graph paper (to help with spacing). Place the lettered paper on a non-slip surface for stability.

3 Cover the letters with fabric and tape down the edges.

4 Rub the flat end of a paint stick or the side of a stick removed from the cardboard sleeve over fabric, picking up the words beneath.

5 Let the design dry and heat set.

With fabric placed on a non-slip surface, place strips of masking tape in a striped or grid pattern. Rub paint stick onto a piece of masking tape or rough paper and then load a stencil brush from the tape or paper. Brush paint over the fabric with the tape acting as a resist. Remove the tape, let the paint dry, and heat set.

Stencils

Sticks and stencils make it easy to add patterns to fabric surfaces. (Stencil by Diane Ericson, ReVisions.)

1 Place the fabric on a non-slip surface. Use tape or spray adhesive to adhere the stencil to the fabric.

2 Rub paint stick onto a piece of masking tape or rough paper and load the stencil brush from the tape or paper. Brush or daub paint into stencil openings. Remove stencil.

3 Another option: If there is space around the edges of stencil openings, rub paint stick onto the plastic edges and drag the paint into the openings, working from the edges to the center to create shading.

4 Let the design dry and heat set.

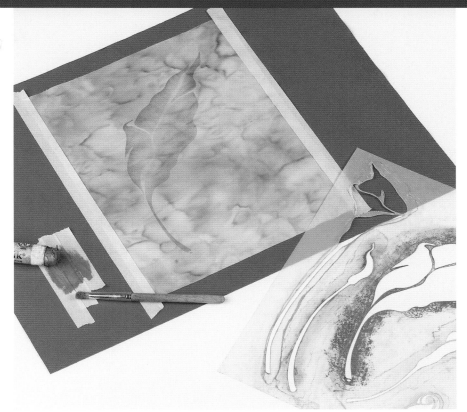

To make a stenciled motif appear three dimensional, use a dark color on one side of the openings and a light color on the other side, as if there was a light source coming from one side. You might want to make the background fabric be the true color of the motif, i.e. green for leaves, for more realism. Stencil by Diane Ericson, ReVisions.

Freezer Paper

To give your appliqué a dimensional look, start with a freezer-paper stencil.

1 Draw a design on freezer paper.

2 Using a craft knife carefully cut out the motif, leaving the margins intact. Use the paper from around the motif to create a shadow for your appliqué.

3 Iron the shiny side of the freezer paper outline to the fabric with a dry iron.

4 Place the fabric on a non-slip surface, rub paint stick on the paper around the opening, and then use a stencil brush to drag the paint onto the fabric. Remove freezer paper.

5 Let the design dry and heat set.

6 Create a raised appliqué that mirrors your stenciled pattern. Iron the freezer paper motif to the right side of the appliqué fabric. You can iron fusible web to the back of the fabric first and cut right on the edge of the pattern. Or add a scant ¼" (6 mm) around the pattern when you cut it out for turn-under seam allowances.

7 Place the appliqué to one side of the paint stick image to create a shadow effect and fuse or stitch down.

Heavy Paper or Cardboard

Make wonderfully soft landscapes using paper and paint sticks.

1 Tear a piece of heavy paper or cardboard into two pieces.

2 Place one of the paper pieces on the fabric and rub paint stick on the rough edges.

3 Drag the paint off the paper onto the fabric with a stencil brush. Move the paper down on the fabric and repeat to create stripes. Use both halves of the paper and turn them over for four different edges.

4 Once you have applied the soft stripes, continue to shade the spaces between them, leaving a bit of the original fabric showing between "mountains." Use the same brush for all the colors to blend them and make them look more natural.

5 Let the design dry and heat set.

Advancing the Stick

If you need to advance the stick to expose more paint, pull the cardboard apart and push the stick up, leaving the cardboard intact so you always have the full-size sleeve to hang onto.

This wall hanging by Sue Kelly started as dyed fabric, which was quilted in a preplanned pattern. Different raised areas were colored with paint stick so that the quilting lines remained the original color of the fabric.

If you love quilting but don't want to do piecing or appliqué, stitch a whole cloth quilt and then remove and add color. In this sample, a black quilted piece was discharged with a mixture of discharge paste and paint; painted with Lumiere metallic paint; and colored with a paint stick. The only original color still showing is seen in the black lines in the recesses of the quilting stitches and the outline on the feathers. Quilting by Sue Kelly.

Screen Printing

Screen printing, or silk screening, allows you to make multiple prints that are exactly the same. It works well for doing t-shirts, posters, or an overall design on yardage. There are several ways to make a screen. Some require access to expensive equipment or chemicals, such as screen filler and drawing fluid. But, for our purposes, we can make screens quickly and easily or purchase thermofax screens, with or without designs.

You can purchase a basic screen with a wooden frame from many art supply stores and then use it with many temporary masks. Buy a size that corresponds to the size of the project you typically make—the screen should be larger than the image size by an inch or two all around. The polyester mesh on the screen should be 10XX to 14XX for fabric. For mediums, choose thicker fabric paint like Neopaque (not metallic), thickened dye, discharge paste or chlorine dishwasher gel (for removing color), or screen printing inks. The medium should have the consistency of pudding or yogurt. You will also need a squeegee, either a wooden handled version with a hard rubber blade or a special plastic one, cut 1" (2.5 cm) narrower than the width of the screen mesh. If you are only doing a small screen, you can use a credit card or other piece of stiff plastic.

Custom-sized Thermofax screens can be made inexpensively. They consist of a plastic-coated mesh that is burned out with an old machine used to make ditto copies. The image can be very detailed, and the screens last for a long time if properly cleaned. You can also tape plain polyester mesh to lightweight plastic Thermofax frames for easily cleaned and stored screens. Screen printing works best if you print on a slightly padded surface. Padded surfaces can be created with rubber carpet padding, batting, newsprint, or terry cloth covered with plastic and a top layer of muslin. Padding materials should be stretched taut on your work surface and free of wrinkles. This surface also serves well for stamping and other printing methods where a little give underneath allows for better contact with the fabric. Practice on scrap fabric to determine the amount of pressure needed to effectively pull the medium over the screen.

YOU WILL NEED

- wooden screen printing frame or canvas stretcher bars and mesh
- duct tape
- adhesive shelf paper
- fabric
- squeegee
- Neopaque paint by Jacquard (see resources)
- masking tape
- scrap paper
- freezer paper
- Elmer's Washable School Glue Gel
- flour
- stencils
- watercolor crayons
- fluid acrylic medium (see resources)
- cleaning brush and liquid cleaner

1

Screen Basics

Prepare a readymade wooden screen for printing, or make your own wooden screen by fitting together four canvas stretcher bars and stapling polyester mesh tautly across the face of the frame.

1 To prepare a wood-framed screen, cover all the wood with duct tape, extending the tape ½" (1.3 cm) onto the mesh on three sides and 1" (2.5 cm) on one end to give you a place to pour the medium.

2 Scour the mesh with an old toothbrush and cleanser. Dry thoroughly.

3 Cut a piece of self-adhesive shelf paper slightly smaller than the outside measurements of your frame.

4 Prepare an image to print by cutting a design into shelf paper cut slightly smaller than the outside measurements of the frame. Keep the design area at least ½" (1.3 cm) smaller than the exposed mesh of the screen.

5 Remove the protective paper on the sticky-back shelf paper. Adhere paper sticky side down on the back of the mesh (the side that will lie flush against the fabric). Rub the plastic firmly onto the mesh.

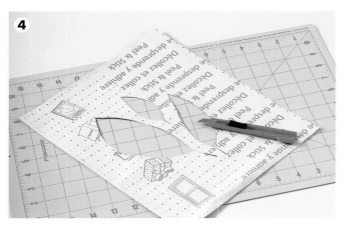

4

The sample shows how the sticky-back plastic-covered screen was used to print onto fabric, which was then quilted. Starting with a batik fabric background adds interest and coordinates with the color of the paint.

Masking Materials

Look to your craft cupboards for supplies that you can use to mask-off patterns to print.

Press masking tape onto the mesh to create a pleasing pattern, set screen over fabric, and squeegee medium over screen. After you finish printing, immediately remove the tape to avoid transferring adhesive.

For a simple, deconstructed print, tear paper and arrange it on the fabric. When you lay the screen over the paper and squeegee medium across it, the paper will temporarily adhere to the bottom of the screen. As you make subsequent prints, the paper will start to fall off, altering each print's appearance.

Make a freezer-paper mask. Stamp or draw an image onto the paper's dull side and cut out the openings for paint to go through. Iron the shiny side carefully to the back of the mesh on the screen.

Use Elmer's Washable School Glue Gel to draw a design onto screen. Let the glue dry thoroughly before using it to make a print. If you do a long series of prints, the glue will start to dissolve and create interesting variations. This sample was done with a partially clogged screen which added texture to the print's background.

Use commercial plastic stencils or paper ones that you cut yourself in a different way. Place stencils on fabric and then cover with the screen. The screen allows you to quickly squeegee medium without catching the squeegee on the stencil's cut-out areas.

Draw motifs on a blank screen with watercolor crayons. Use fluid acrylic as the printing medium and do several prints on top of each other, moving the screen between prints. The crayon lines will last through many prints.

Printing Methods

1 Tape fabric to the print table so you can lift off the screen without moving the fabric. You will probably not get a perfect print the first time (the screen needs to absorb some of the medium) so have a second fabric piece ready to print. If you plan to print several pieces, tape them in place so you can move quickly from one to the next.

2 To make a print with any of the screens above, pour a line of ink, paint, discharge agent, or other print-apt medium on the tape at the top of the screen. Pour two or three colors side-by-side if desired; the colors will mix as you squeegee the paint across.

3 Hold the screen tightly or have someone else hold it and firmly pull the squeegee and medium across the screen. Experiment with the squeegee angle. You should be able to print the design with one pass but if you need a second pass, scoop up the excess paint at the bottom of the screen with the squeegee and start again at the top. Work quickly so the medium does not dry on the screen.

4 After printing, immediately wash the screen with a brush and liquid cleanser to open the holes in the mesh.

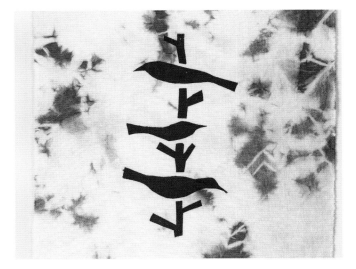

Less Than Perfect

Screen printing is fun and easy to do, but rarely results in a perfect print unless you practice often and find a medium that suits the way you work. Be patient and consider printed imperfections part of the process. When you sew the print into a project, minor imperfections can be stitched around to define them or partially hidden with a sprinkled application of foil.

Foiling

Foiling adds a beautiful shine that is not achievable with metallic paint and provides a wonderful accent and depth to surface design techniques already on the fabric. The fabric below was first painted with a masking tape resist, potato printed, overlaid with painted Misty Fuse, and then foiled.

Be sure you purchase foil intended for fabric and experiment with different kinds of adhesives. The foil will stick wherever you apply adhesive. Some adhesives to try are Foil Transfer Adhesive from Laura Murray Designs (liquid), Foil Glue by Jones Tones (liquid), Bo-Nash Bonding Agent (granules), Wonder-Under by Pellon (paper-backed web), Misty Fuse (web), other fusible webs, YLI fusible thread, and glue sticks and glue gun. Once your fabric is foiled, wash it and hang to dry. Do not dry clean it. As long as you protect the foiled areas when pressing a garment or project, the foil will be quite durable.

Continue to use the foil sheets until there is no color left. Sometimes lighter applications of foil are very attractive so partially used sheets are useful. Also, if a part of the design is missed by one sheet, you can use a second sheet of color to add accents. Using a lightweight iron with a non-stick surface helps make the burnishing process easier and avoids build-up of adhesive or foil on the iron's sole plate.

YOU WILL NEED

- Foil Transfer Adhesive (see resources)
- rubber stamps
- sponge brush
- foil sheets (see resources)
- Bo-Nash Bonding Agent
- Wonder-Under fusible web
- Misty Fuse adhesive web
- parchment paper
- fusible thread and cotton thread
- sewing machine
- Jones Tones Foil Glue
- glue gun and glue

Foil Transfer Adhesive

1 Use a sponge brush to coat a rubber stamp with Foil Transfer Adhesive, and stamp adhesive onto fabric. Reload the stamp each time you use it. When you're done stamping, immediately wash the stamp and sponge brush.

2 Let the adhesive dry for 2 or more hours. Cover the dry adhesive with a foil sheet, color side up, and burnish the foil sheet with the edge of the dry iron three or four times to transfer foil.

3 Check to see that the foil has transferred and remove the foil sheet.

Granular Bonding Agent

1 Sprinkle Bo-Nash Bonding Agent on the fabric.

2 Cover granules with cooking parchment and iron until granules melt. Remove the parchment.

3 Cover the adhesive with a foil sheet, color side up, and burnish the foil sheet with the edge of the iron to transfer foil.

4 Check to see that the foil has transferred and remove the foil sheet.

Fusible Webs

1 Cut a shape out of Wonder-Under or other fusible web.

2 Place the shape web side down on the fabric. Iron with a dry iron over the paper, let cool, and peel off the paper.

3 Cover the adhesive remaining on fabric with a foil sheet, color side up, and burnish the foil sheet with the edge of the iron to transfer foil.

4 Check to see that the foil has transferred and remove the foil sheet.

Misty Fuse

1 Cut a shape out of Misty Fuse.

2 Place the shape on the fabric, cover with parchment, and iron. Remove the parchment.

3 Cover the adhesive with a foil sheet, color side up, and burnish the foil sheet with the edge of the iron to transfer foil.

4 Check to see that the foil has transferred and remove the foil sheet.

Fusible Thread

1 Wind fusible thread on the bobbin of a sewing machine and place a spool of cotton thread on the machine's top spindle.

2 Place fabric on machine; sew from the back of the fabric so the fusible thread is on the fabric's right side.

3 Cover the thread with a foil sheet, color side up, and burnish the foil sheet with the edge of the iron to transfer foil to stitches.

4 Check to see that the foil has transferred and remove the foil sheet.

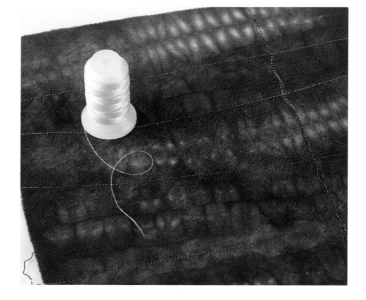

Foil Glue Bottles

1 Use the nozzle on a bottle of Jones Tones Foil Glue to draw a design or words onto fabric. Let the design dry for one to eight hours (glue will turn clear).

2 Place a foil sheet, color side up, over the glue, which will still be tacky. Rub your finger over the sheet to transfer the foil. (This method gives a very dimensional effect.)

3 Check to see that foil has transferred and remove foil sheet.

Glue Sticks and Glue Gun

Use a glue gun to make decorative elements that you can attach to your fabric.

1 With a glue gun, draw designs on the back (dull side) of the foil sheet. Let the glue cool and peel the element off the foil sheet.

2 To attach the element to fabric, lay it right side down on a piece of cooking parchment. Lay the fabric face down over the element and briefly iron until you see the glue coming through the fabric. Do not iron too long or the element will melt.

Test

You will get a sharper foiled image on smoother fabrics, but foil transfers will work on anything. If the foil sheet melts, turn down the iron. Make test samples before beginning a project.

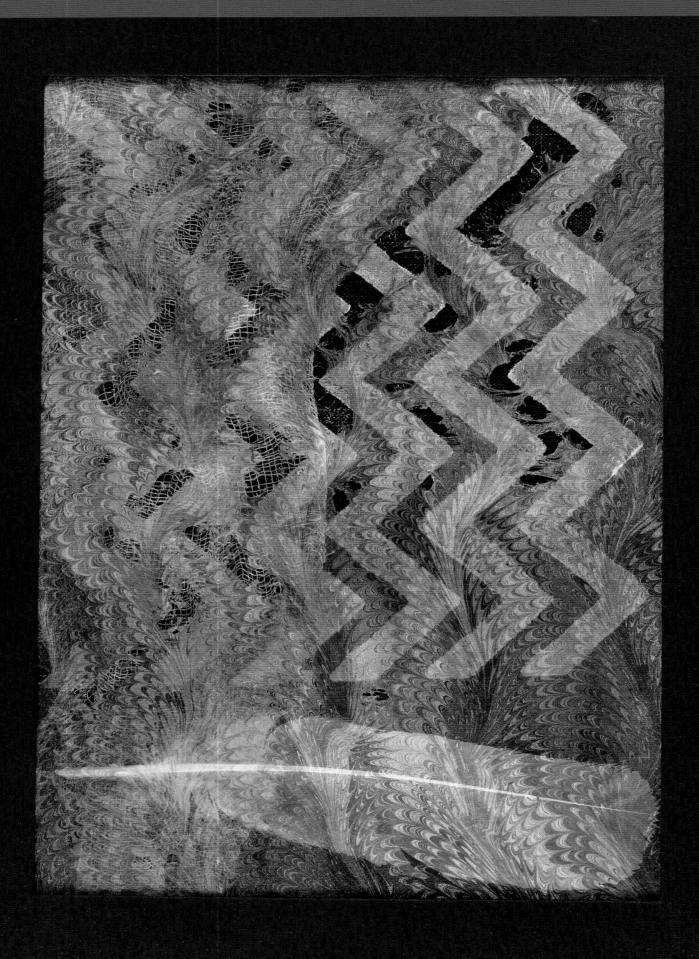

Expandable Paint

Not the puff paint of the seventies, today's expandable paint allows artists to easily apply considerable dimensionality, in several colors, on fabric.

Expandable paint can be applied with a brush, through a stencil, or with a rubber stamp. While wet or dry, the paint is heated with a heat gun or hair dryer and magically expands. It can be colored with paints or pigment powders before it is applied to the fabric or colored afterward with a wash of transparent paint or with brushed-on opaque paints, paint sticks, or other coloring agents. Expandable paint will feel rubbery on the fabric but will not stiffen the fabric and can still be stitched over.

You might want to use a little heavier weight of fabric so it doesn't shrink up too much when heated. Make sure whatever textile you use will not melt—unless you want it to!

Marbled fabric by Mary Holland. This piece was stenciled with expandable paint, heated with a heat gun, colored with Dye-na-Flow paint, foiled, draped with painted cheesecloth, and decorated with a real feather. A layer of Misty Fuse was added, and then hand-marbled nylon organdy was fused on top. The heat gun was used to melt away some of the organdy to reveal underlying layers.

Expandable Paint Techniques

1 Use a sponge brush and Pebeo Expandable Paint and freehand strokes to paint on white fabric.

2 Fuse a piece of heavy lace onto the fabric and paint over the lace, filling some of the spaces with paint.

3 Apply paint to a rubber stamp and stamp a motif onto the fabric.

4 Stencil a design onto the fabric using paint and a sponge brush.

5 Place the fabric on a heat-resistant surface. Hold a heat gun or hair dryer 2" to 3" (5 to 7 cm) above the fabric and use it to dry and expand the paint. If the fabric starts to pucker too much, pin fabric edges to the heat-resistant surface.

Use Dye-na-Flow or other thin paint to paint a wash of color over the expanded paint. Notice the interesting effects as the expandable paint contrasts at different levels with the background. You can also paint over the expandable paint before it is heated.

Apply expandable paint with various methods to a piece of white fabric. Heat the paint until it is expanded. Use paints with different viscosities to discover which effects you like best. Here, five different Jacquard fabric paints are illustrated: Dye na Flow (1), Sorbet (2), Textile color (3), Lumiere (4), and Neopaque (5).

Apply expandable paint to black fabric. Here, the paint was applied with a rubber stamp, stencil, over lace, and brushed on heavily and textured with a comb. Add beads while the paint is wet if you like. Puff up the paint and then color with paint stick and a stencil brush or with metallic or thin paint and a sponge brush. After the paint is dry, foil over the raised surfaces (center sample).

Color can be added to the expandable paint before it is applied. Here, Lumiere metallic paint was added before painting onto black fabric. There is some evidence of the paint's metallic quality but much less than when it is applied afterward. The expandable paint will make any coloring agent more pastel.

Paint a Landscape

Use expandable paint to create naturally textured backdrops, such as sandy beaches, leafy trees, and roughened rocks.

1 Choose a background fabric that replicates the colors of sky or sand or other natural backdrops.

2 Tape fabric to a piece of cardboard and heavily apply expandable paint to fabric.

3 Comb through the paint to create the look of tree bark, embed leaf beads into paint to mimic tree canopies, or embed shells in paint to fashion a sandy beach.

4 Heat and color the paint while the fabric is attached to the cardboard.

Use the fine-point tip built into Jones Tones Ultra-Paint Puff to draw designs onto fabric. Draw a frame around a cut-out motif or write a message in script. This paint comes in an array of colors, which allows you to use expanded-paint images with more saturated colors than those created with Pebeo paint. Let the paint dry and use a heat gun to expand the paint.

Clean Up

After painting, immediately clean your brushes, stamps, stencils, and other tools because expandable paint dries quickly and is permanent once it dries.

Paper-Cloth Layering

Paper-cloth layering is much like a collage process, where you use a variety of materials. Instead of sewing or fusing these elements together, you use an acrylic medium to adhere everything into a single paper sheet.

This piece started with a sheer curtain fabric printed with flowers and leaves.

Choose a theme or color scheme for your fabric layers. Write bold text on Beijie paper or water-soluble paper so text is visible when integrated into the layering. Always use non-bleeding materials, unless that is an effect you want to promote. It is surprising how well various elements integrate with each other: a photo printed on organza laid on top of the collage may be almost obliterated by cheesecloth or Chinese calligraphy paper placed underneath. Note that paper-cloth sheets will be stiff but are easy to sew through. Use your paper-cloth sheets to make gift boxes and bags and to provide focal points in wall hangings. Of course, the layered sheets may also be matted and framed.

Paper-Cloth Layering Basics

1 Lay a piece of smooth plastic or freezer paper (shiny side up) on the table and tape down the edges.

2 With a 3" (7.5 cm) bristle brush, coat the paper or plastic with fluid acrylic medium. Use matte formula if you do not want the piece to be shiny.

3 Rip or roughly cut a piece of sheer fabric or cheesecloth and press it into the medium with the brush or with your hands until it is flat and saturated.

4 Cover the surface with bits of torn paper, photos printed on sheer organza, lacy handmade paper, Chinese Beijie or calligraphy paper, or pieces of sheer silk.

5 Coat each addition with more acrylic medium and rub into the surface. When layering is complete (ah, there is the question!), leave the laid-flat piece to dry.

The support for layers can be on top of the piece, instead of being the first layer. Lay cut or torn paper, odds and ends of fabric, and other embellishments on the layer of acrylic medium. Cover with a large piece of sheer fabric or cheesecloth and saturate with more medium, rubbing it in with your hands. Piece made by Mary B. Johnson.

Chinese papers may mush up if rubbed too much, but the irregular mushy surface can expand your creative options. Draw with crayons on Beijie paper or paint it with textile paint. When the torn pieces of paper are added to the layering, only the painting and drawing will show. Piece made by Mary B. Johnson.

Take It Further

Paint on the paper-cloth, sew into it with machine or hand stitching, or add more elements with the fluid acrylic medium. Cut the piece up and sew it onto a fabric background, decorating it with beads or ribbon.

Angelina

Angelina fiber is a synthetic fiber, sold either as film or as straight cuts and crimped shreds. A ½-ounce bag goes a long way, but you can buy assortment packs and get small amounts of many colors. Be sure you always buy "hot fix" fiber. Some metallic fibers, including Mylar, will not bond together to make a flat sheet. A small amount of other fibers can be mixed with Angelina, which will fuse everything together. Angelina will not fuse to fabric unless you include a layer of Misty Fuse on the bottom when you iron the sheet. You can also attach Angelina to fabric with stitches or by trapping it behind netting. Of course, you can use Angelina fiber in silk fusion or other projects without making it into sheets—just don't apply too much heat or the color of the Angelina will change.

When making Angelina sheets, protect your iron to prevent making a big mess. Cooking parchment or the release paper from fusible web works well as a protective layer between iron and Angelina; the pressing paper can be thrown away as soon as it gets sticky. It doesn't hurt to put parchment under the Angelina to protect the ironing board cover, although there shouldn't be a bond.

Three factors determine the final color and sheen of an Angelina sheet: iron temperature, the time iron is pressed to Angelina, and the amount of pressure applied to the iron. Experiment to see how your iron works with Angelina and what you need to do to get the desired look. Angelina will lose its sheen fairly quickly and will eventually turn brown if you leave the iron on long enough. After the project is completed, be aware that any pressing you do will continue to alter the Angelina.

YOU WILL NEED

- Angelina hot fix shreds (see resources)
- Angelina film (see resources)
- cooking parchment
- iron
- foam stamp
- fabrics
- Misty Fuse adhesive web
- foil (see resources)

Angelina Shreds

1 Place some loose shreds, either plain or crimped, on a piece of cooking parchment.

2 Cover with another sheet of parchment and press for a few seconds. Check that the shreds are bonded together and are still shiny. If they are dull, start again, using a lower iron temperature.

3 Remove the parchment and allow the bonded sheet to cool.

4 Cut the bonded sheet into squares or strips and sprinkle them on top of a fresh pile of shreds in a contrasting color. Cover with parchment and press.

Stamp Impressions

Various amounts of heating time will result in: a perfect impression; an impression dulled from being too "cooked" (a creative design option); an impression that is burned, which can be attractive as a contrast to uncooked Angelina; and Angelina and a stamp destroyed by too much heat. So many choices! These samples show the results of several different "cooking" times.

1 Cover a foam stamp with shreds in an even layer. Cover with cooking parchment and set a hot iron on top for a few seconds.

2 Cool and remove the paper and Angelina from the stamp.

Weaving

Use Angelina shreds and fusible web to make a woven piece that can be bonded to fabric.

1 Layer parchment, Misty Fuse web, two or more colors of Angelina shreds to cover the web, and parchment.

2 Press lightly with iron and check to see that the Misty Fuse has bonded to the back of the Angelina.

3 Cut the sheet of Angelina into strips and loosely weave strips together.

4 Lay the weaving on a piece of black fabric and cover with parchment. Flip pieces over and iron from the back just until the weaving fuses to the fabric—too much ironing time will change the color of the Angelina.

Film Techniques

1 Lay a piece of black fabric on top of a foam stamp, then a piece of Misty Fuse, a piece of Angelina film, and cover everything with parchment.

2 Heat with the iron until the film is embossed with the stamp's pattern. Remove the stamp. Iron layers again to fasten the film edges to the fabric. For more durability, stitch around the edges of the film.

Scrunch a piece of film very tightly and then lightly iron it between sheets of parchment. The wrinkling adds more iridescence. When moved, this piece shows copper, green, blue, and pink shimmers. Use the piece as a pocket, a collage overlay, or fairy or dragonfly wings. Another way to add texture is to aim a heat gun at a plain piece of film, which causes the film to bubble and curl. As always, use precautions to avoid breathing fumes.

This charming fairy, made by Pam Ehlers-Stec using a Rick Petersen pattern, has Angelina film wings. Thin wires were bent into the shape of the wings, covered on both sides with film, and heated until the film melted onto the wires and developed holes. See more at mysweetcherryblossom.blogspot.com

In case Angelina film doesn't supply enough glitz, iron a piece of Misty Fuse web onto black fabric with cooking parchment placed on top to protect the iron. Remove parchment. Iron foil onto the Misty Fuse. Iron another color of foil onto the Angelina film (no adhesive needed) and then iron the film onto the Misty Fuse with parchment placed on top to protect the iron.

Try This

Use Angelina sheets or loose Angelina fibers to represent reflections or light sources in landscape appliqués.

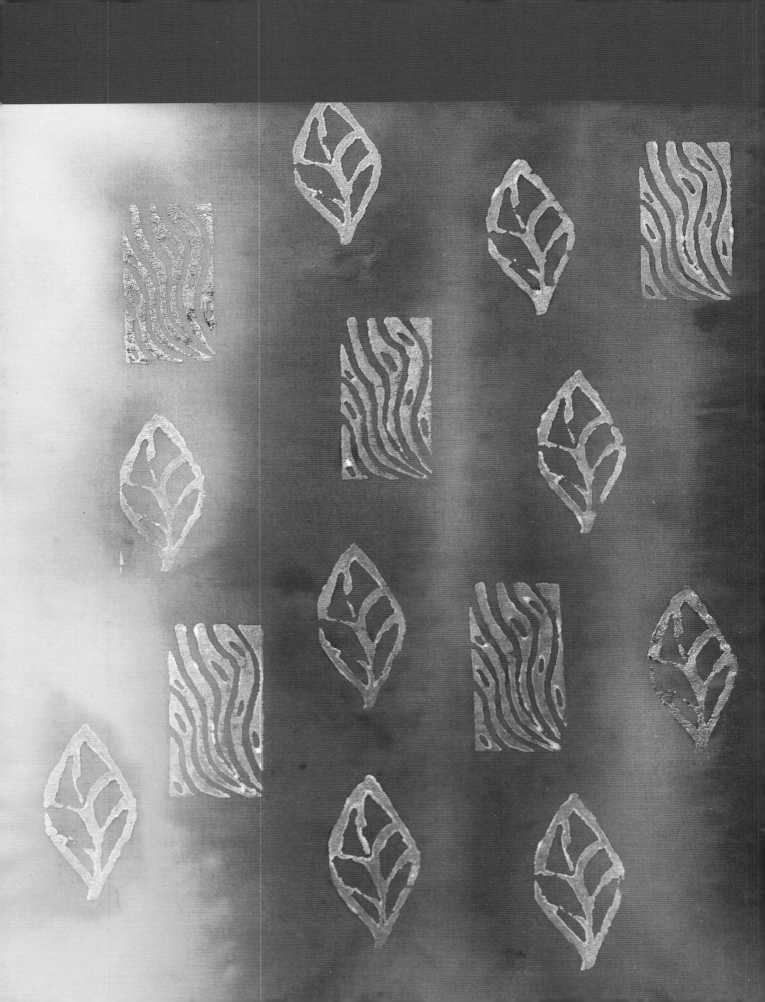

Stamping

One of the handiest ways to get images onto fabric is stamping because stamping tools—kitchen utensils, kids' toys, natural objects, fruits and vegetables, to-go boxes, erasers, corks, buttons, and foam sheets—are always within reach.

There are also the rubber, acrylic, and sponge stamps we all collect and purchase at craft and decorating stores. You can use thickened dye, discharge agents, paints of a thicker viscosity, and inks as mediums. How you load the stamping device varies too—use a sponge or sponge brush, a brayer, paint spread on plastic or glass, or a commercial or homemade ink pad.

Repeat images over and over to create a piece of yardage, or stamp one image to create a focal point. Re-load the stamp each time you make an image for a bolder look, or do a second print without re-loading the stamp for a more subtle look. Work on a surface padded with a towel, old mouse pad, or newspaper to create clearer prints. Make a first print onto paper to prime the stamp; take care to keep medium from getting into the negative areas of the stamp.

These two designs were cut by friends and then stamped onto fabric using expandable paint. The paint was heated to puff it up, and then a wash of Dye-na-Flow paint was used to fill in the background. Finally, foil was used to embellish two of the prints without using additional adhesive.

Stamp-Loading Basics

1 Use a sponge or sponge brush to load any stamp with medium. The sponge will give a different texture than a sponge brush, since brushstrokes will be inevitable and visible.

2 Or, use a brayer to spread paint onto a piece of plastic or glass and then load the stamp with the medium-coated brayer or directly from medium on the glass.

3 Use ink pads. Make sure commercial pads contain permanent ink that will work on fabric. Make your own ink pad by pouring paint onto a folded paper towel. Paint or dye should be thick enough so it doesn't bleed out from the stamped image; use thinner mediums to create a watercolor effect.

Other Options

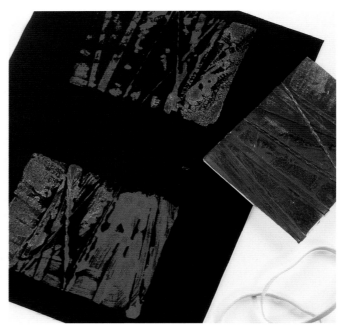

Make a string stamp. Wrap string around a piece of acrylic, wood, or cardboard. Tape the string to the back of a stamp to keep the string from slipping. To make a very sharp print, use a brayer to ink the stamp so the medium only coats the string. Here the string stamp was loaded using a sponge brush, which created a slightly less defined print.

Make a rubber band stamp. Wrap rubber bands around a piece of foam core or cardboard. Load with paint and stamp on top of the fabric to create a less filled-in print, or place the stamp on the table, place the fabric on top, and rub over fabric with your fingers to get more coverage.

Vary the view. Load a rubber band stamp and print onto one fabric; then, without adding more paint, use the stamp to print onto a second fabric. The two prints will coordinate, but look considerably different.

Make a bubble wrap stamp. Wrap bubble wrap around a piece of acrylic or foam core and tape to the back. Make a duct-tape handle for ease of stamping. Peel one layer off a piece of corrugated cardboard, leaving some of the outer layer on if desired. Load the bubble wrap or cardboard with medium and stamp onto fabric.

Make etched stamps. With a ballpoint pen, etch lines into a meat tray or to-go box. Load with paint or other medium and stamp onto fabric. Go back and add more paint with a sponge brush if desired.

Make stamps from foam. Use adhesive-backed foam door insulation to make a stamp design and stick it to a piece of acrylic. Cut designs from adhesive-backed foam sheets from the craft store and stick them to wall insulation board, foam core, or cardboard. Even kids' foam stickers work well for making a quick stamp. For ease of handling, add a duct tape handle to the back. On the leaf sample pictured here, a sponge brush was used to create subtle vein markings in the paint as it was applied to the stamp.

Make stamps from almost anything. Use a pencil eraser as a stamp to add dotted interest to a small quilt. Glue a button to the end of a spool, film canister, or pill bottle for a unique stamp. Carve a wine-bottle cork into a simple shape. Look at kids' toys for flat shapes that can be used as stamps. Use your imagination to come up with other options.

Make an impression. Buy foam that can be heated and then impressed with the shape of any hard object. Use this technique to make a negative of a rubber stamp that can be used to create complex designs on fabric. Make sure the item that will be impressed in the foam is deep enough to make a sharp impression.

Print with mesh and fencing. Place rug gripper mesh or a piece of construction fence on a protected surface, roll over it with a loaded brayer, and use the coated piece as a stamp. If you put mesh on top of fabric while you are loading the mesh, the fabric underneath will also be colored. Turn the coated mesh over onto a second piece of fabric to print; work very quickly so the paint does not dry on the mesh.

Vary the view. Use mesh as a mask when stamping. Place it over the fabric, tape it around the edges, and then use another stamp to make images on the fabric, which will be interrupted by the mesh.

Artist's Eraser

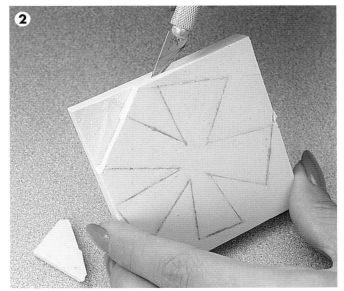

1 Make a stamp from a white eraser or larger pieces of white rubber available at art supply stores. Draw a design onto the eraser and use a craft knife to cut about ¼" (6mm) deep along the design lines.

2 To create raised stamp edges, cut horizontally into the eraser, moving up the first cuts and removing the background. For other areas, cut at an angle along the design and remove the excess rubber.

Or, use a linoleum cutter to carve out a design in an eraser. This will create a more primitive, wood-cut look. Glue erasers to acrylic or wood to make them easier to use.

Layers

Remember that stamping is only the beginning. Add a second layer of stamping to increase interest and depth and then stitch, foil, or otherwise embellish the fabric.

Rust Dyeing

Rust dyeing is a beautiful way to create patterns and is easy to do.

All you need is an item that will rust, fabric, vinegar, and a little time.

The process will work on silk and cotton—just make sure fabric is free of sizing and finishes. Look for old pieces of metal, steel wool, washers, nails, springs, gears, architectural elements, grates, and metal filings. Buying new items may prove fruitless as everything is now made NOT to rust!

YOU WILL NEED

- tray
- fabrics
- vinegar
- spray bottle
- steel wool
- wire that will rust
- washers and other metal objects
- refrigerator magnets
- metal filings
- large plastic bags
- salt

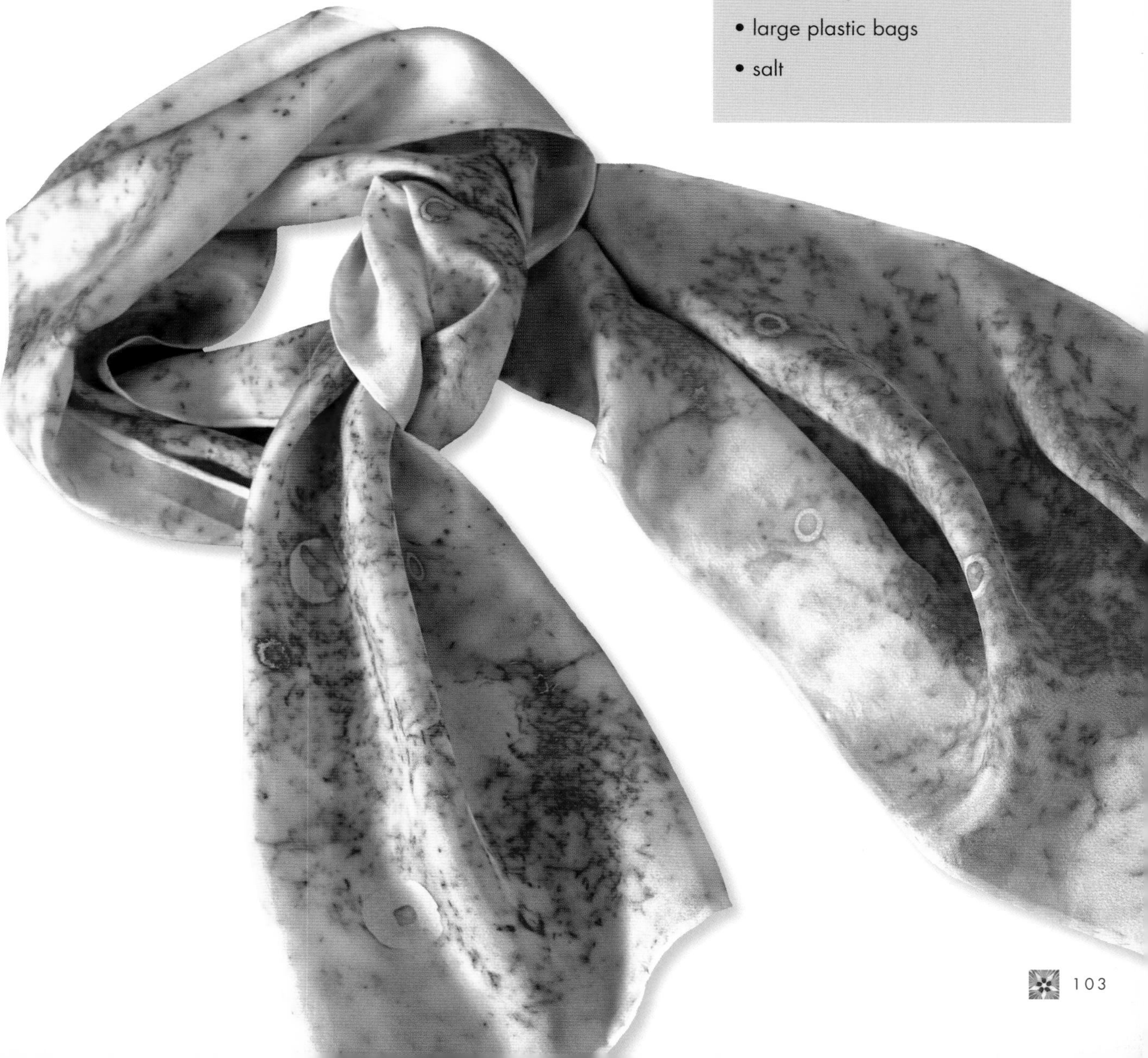

Rust Dyeing Basics

1 Lay fabric on a tray or cookie sheet (if the tray or cookie sheet is rusty, all the better).

2 Spray the fabric with a half and half mix of vinegar and water and then cover fabric with steel wool and other metal objects. Use caution when handling already rusty items and do not breathe in their dust. Spray the fabric again.

3 Slip the filled tray into a plastic garbage bag and tie the bag's end. Weigh down the top of bag with books to make sure the metal items are tight to the fabric.

4 Let bag sit for up to 24 hours in a warm place. (The process may not take that long.)

5 Uncover the fabric and neutralize it with ¼ cup (60 mL) of salt mixed into four gallons (16 L) of water. Wash the fabric with soap and water.

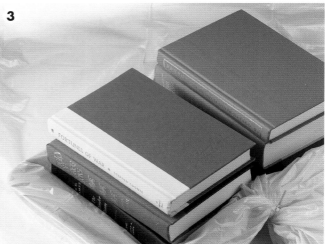

Thinking Big

If you have a large metal object like a tractor gear, place the fabric on a piece of thick foam, spray with vinegar-water, and then place the metal object on the fabric. It will sink into the foam, pressing the metal against the fabric. Place the whole thing in plastic to process.

Look for specially cut shapes or wire guaranteed to rust (see resources). Twist wire into shapes or words, keeping wire as flat as possible, before placing it on the fabric. Spray with vinegar water and seal inside a plastic bag.

Cut refrigerator magnets into shapes and sprinkle them with metal filings. Cover with fabric and spray with vinegar-water. Seal in plastic to process.

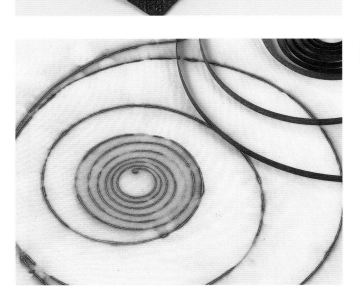

Ask repair shops to save old parts that you can use in your dyeing efforts. This spring is from a chain saw. The spring was placed between two pieces of white fabric that were dyed at the same time. See the finished piece at the beginning of this chapter.

Altered Lutrador and Heavy Interfacings

Lutrador is an interfacing used in industrial applications, such as auto upholstery. It comes in varying thicknesses and is valued because it takes color well, looks organic even though it is polyester, and can be melted with a heat gun or heat tool (like a soldering iron).

Use any paint, ink, or other coloring agent as long as it will color synthetic material. Leave the medium in place to dry; blotting the medium with a paper towel will remove most of the color.

Peltex and Timtex are very heavy weight interfacings used to shore up baseball-cap brims and for creating fabric art projects, such as fabric bowls. They both melt and can be cut into with a heat tool, making it easy to create fanciful edges, windows, even script. Fast2Fuse interfacing is the same weight as Peltex and Timtex, but it has fusible adhesive on both sides so you won't need to use Misty Fuse or Wonder-Under to attach additional elements.

YOU WILL NEED

- Lutrador interfacing (see resources)
- Peltex, Fast2Fuse, or Timtex heavy duty interfacing
- Dye-na-Flow paint
- Misty Fuse adhesive web
- Wonder-Under fusible web
- glass piece
- heat tool and heat gun
- thin paints or inks
- sponge brushes
- cooking parchment
- foil for fabric
- freezer paper
- masking tape
- spray adhesive
- metal stencil
- novelty fabrics
- fabric glue
- natural items or button
- synthetic felt

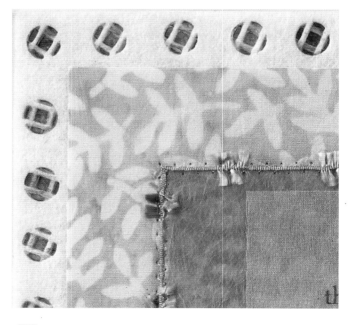

> Every woman
> should develop
> the kinds of bonds
> that will allow her to know
> she has someone
> she can count on.
>
> Someone who will give her
> the best advice,
> even if it is unpleasant.
> Someone who will expect
> the most from her...
>
> and someone with whom
> she can
> celebrate life.
>
> Maya Angelou

This piece has a photo of a sunset over the ocean printed onto Lutrador that was backed with freezer paper. The Lutrador was fused to fabric with Misty Fuse web, and the fabric was fused to Peltex interfacing with Wonder-Under web. A Maya Angelou quote was printed onto ExtravOrganza inkjet fabric and the fabric was fused atop the Lutrador. The Peltex was embossed with a decorative heat tool, which burned a brown color into the border as it melted a pattern into the interfacing.

Layered Note Card

Make a cheerful little note, created from two pieces of Fast2Fuse painted with diluted Dye-na-Flow.

1 Cut two lengths of interfacing. The top piece should be smaller than the bottom piece because you will want to see much of the bottom piece in the final design.

2 Dampen interfacing and paint it with a sponge brush. Allow plenty of time for the pieces to dry.

3 Place the pieces on a piece of glass with masking-taped edges. With a burning tool (a soldering iron or a decorative heat tool by Walnut Hollow), cut through interfacing with the tool's hot point.

4 Stack the two pieces, smallest on top, cover with cooking parchment, and fuse the two pieces together (the adhesive still works even after being painted).

5 Fuse a piece cut from novelty fabric on top; foil exposed Fast2Fuse if desired.

Computer Printer

Use a computer and printer to transfer digital images to Lutrador. Photos will be lighter colored when printed so choose images accordingly.

1 Cut 8½" x 11" (20.5 x 28 cm) pieces of Lutrador and freezer paper. Use an iron to fuse Lutrador to freezer paper.

2 Place masking tape around top edge of Lutrador/paper sheet so printer can grab paper. Print image on sheet.

3 After printing and allowing image to dry, peel off the freezer paper.

Make a Book

Create a book from embellished Lutrador pages. Since Lutrador will not tear and softens with use, books can withstand lots of wear and tear.

1 Cut three 8" by 16" (20.5 x 40.5 cm) pieces of Lutrador. Sew them together along the center and fold in half to make a book.

2 Paint the pages before or after sewing them together. Let paint dry.

3 Fuse shapes cut from fabric or magazine pages and photo transfers onto each page. Cut or melt off the interfacing along the top and/or side edges of the images.

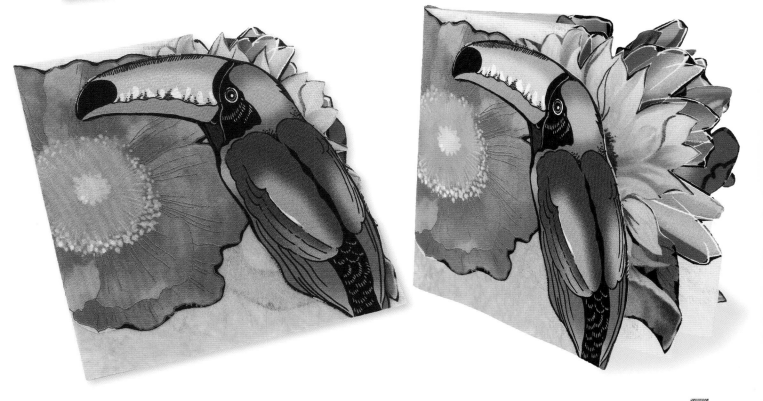

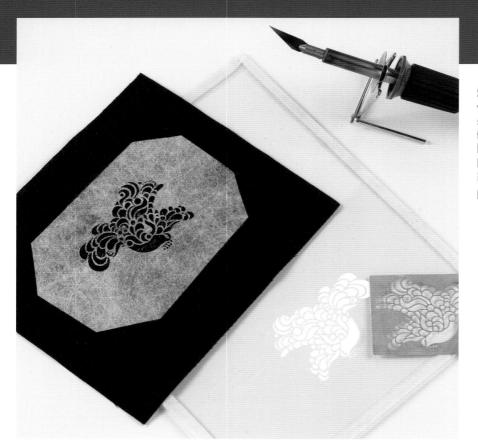

Spray the back of a metal stencil with adhesive, let it dry, and then stick stencil to a piece of Lutrador taped onto glass. Use a heat tool to burn the stencil's open areas into the Lutrador. Use Misty Fuse to fuse the interfacing to fabric and color the piece(s) with paint or ink.

Layered Frame

Build a fabric frame from interfacing squares. Make the squares as large as you like and cut as many windows as space allows. (Felted button by Pat Grady, www.em-bliss.com)

1 Paint four 6" (15 cm) squares of Peltex or Timtex with different colors of diluted Dye-na-Flow and let dry.

2 Determine order in which squares will be layered. From painted squares, cut squares that will be 1" (2.5 cm) smaller than the one placed underneath: 6" (15 cm), 5" (12.5 cm), 4" (10 cm), and 3" (7.5 cm).

3 Glue top three squares together with fabric glue and cover with heavy books until glue dries.

4 Use a heat tool to cut a window through the three layers.

5 Glue the bottom square (I painted the outer edges a darker color than the center) to the pile.

6 Center a shell, rock, or other object in the window and glue to bottom square.

Cut a piece of printed fabric slightly smaller than a piece of synthetic felt and fuse together. Cut a piece of Lutrador to the same size as printed fabric and paint with Dye-na-Flow; let dry. Stitch across the Lutrador, fabric, and felt, outlining some of the printed fabric's motifs as you work. With a heat gun, melt away some of the Lutrador to reveal bits of the printed fabric and to distress the felt.

Safety

Always work outdoors or in a well-ventilated area when burning synthetics. Use a respirator if you must work indoors.

Gelatin Printing

Gelatin printing is a variation of monoprinting, meaning one print per setup, but you can often get a second print that is lighter than the first.

The gelatin pad used to apply thickened dye, ink, or paint is an ideal surface on which to manipulate mediums and it feels delicious on your hands, especially on a hot day. A gelatin pad allows the medium to stay moist longer and creates excellent detail in contrast to medium applied to a piece of glass or plastic, which dries very quickly, is rigid and slippery, and may not hold or release all details.

Medium can be applied to the pad with a brayer, a sponge or sponge brush, or a rubber stamp. A second print can be brought out by spraying the medium-coated pad with water. The gelatin will stand up to several hours of printing before being returned to the refrigerator for another day's artistry. If the gelatin breaks up, spread out the pieces and continue printing for dramatic results.

YOU WILL NEED

- Knox unflavored gelatin, one package
- 8" (20.5 cm) or 9" (23 cm) cake pan
- fabric paint or thickened dye
- rubber stamps
- sponges and sponge brushes
- resists like netting, fencing, and stencils
- bubble wrap and plastic wrap
- fabric
- combing tool or cotton swabs

Make a gelatin print pad by dissolving four envelopes of unflavored gelatin in a cup of cold water. Add a cup of hot water and stir until granules dissolve (be careful not to make bubbles as you stir). Let the gelatin set up in an 8" (20.5 cm) or 9" (23 cm) cake pan. Run a knife around pan edges, pop gelatin round onto a piece of plastic wrap, and you're ready to go.

Resists

1 Apply paint to gelatin's surface with a sponge, sponge brush, or brayer.

2 Lay a piece of rug gripper, construction fencing, a paper or plastic stencil, plastic mesh bag, torn paper, leaf, or sequin waste on top of the paint. The resist must have holes so the fabric can pick up paint. This will be a negative print; the design will remain the fabric's original color and the background will print.

3 Drop a piece of fabric on top of the resist and rub over the fabric's back side with your hands.

4 Carefully pull the fabric up and set aside to dry.

(Continued)

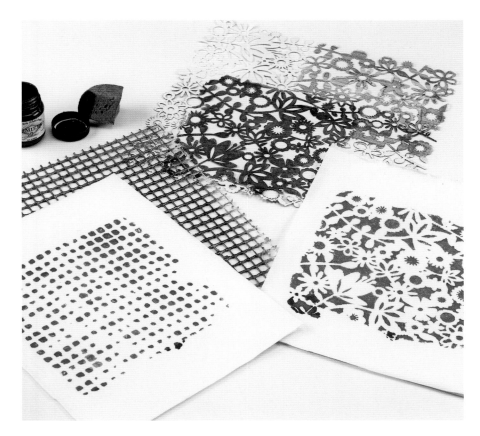

(Continued)

5 Make a positive print. Pull the resist off the gelatin and quickly drop it, medium side facing up, onto the plastic-covered table. Cover resist with a piece of fabric, rub over back of fabric, and pull off fabric. Set fabric aside to dry.

6 Make another positive. Quickly drop a third piece of fabric onto the gelatin and rub over it to create a positive print of the resist. (Three prints for the price of one!)

5

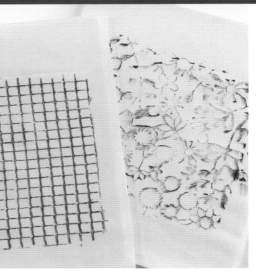

6

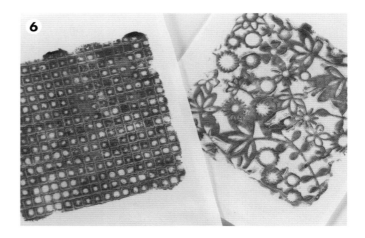

Apply medium to the gelatin and remove some of it with bubble wrap or scrunched up plastic wrap. Drop fabric on the gelatin and rub over the back with your hands. Pull the fabric up and set aside.

Load a rubber stamp with medium and stamp medium onto the gelatin. Drop a piece of fabric onto the gelatin and rub over the back; in addition to stamped image, you will also pick up leftover paint from the previous print. You may be able to get a second print, called a ghost print, by misting the gelatin with water and dropping a second piece of fabric on top.

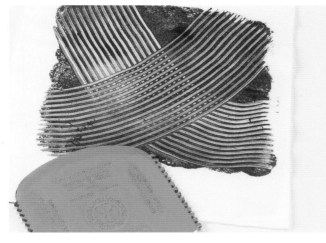

Paint the gelatin with medium and draw into it with a combing tool, cotton swab, or other device. Drop a piece of fabric onto the gelatin, rub, and pull off.

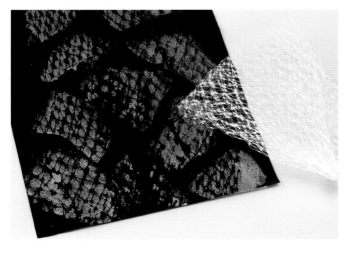

Tear the gelatin apart and rearrange on the plastic. Paint the pieces with medium, cover with resists, and print fabric as before.

Cleaning the Gelatin

Don't clean the gelatin after each print—the excess paint will contribute nice accents to the next print. If you do clean the gelatin, be very careful not to tear it or gouge the surface. If imperfections occur, get creative and use them as design elements.

Sun Printing

Sun printing is easy and magical. Fabric is painted with transparent paint like Dye-na-Flow, objects are laid on top, and the sun prints the objects onto the cloth.

Areas underneath placed items will be lighter and areas exposed to the sun will be brighter or darker. Lots of things, including leaves, feathers, rice and pasta, kids' letters, paper or plastic stencils, paper cutouts, cheesecloth, and wrinkles in the fabric, make great masks for printing. If the sun isn't cooperative the day you want to print, use halogen lights. Choose fabric that is tightly woven and a light color. Choose paint colors that are dark for more contrast.

YOU WILL NEED

- light-colored fabrics
- plastic covered foam core board
- Dye-na-Flow paint in dark colors
- sponge brushes
- masking tape
- netting to hold things in place
- stencils
- scrapbooking cut-out sheets
- cheesecloth
- sunlight or halogen lights

This piece is sun printed with rice and then bordered with a commercial sun print done many yards at a time.

Sun Printing Basics

1 Place fabric on a portable waterproof surface, like plastic-covered foam core board. Tape fabric edges to board and spray with water.

2 Paint Dye-na-Flow paint all over the fabric; use as many colors as desired but work quickly as only wet paint will print.

3 Lay objects on the wet paint, making sure they are as flush to the fabric as possible. Set the fabric in direct sun. If it is breezy, weigh down objects with marbles or rocks or cover the entire board with fine netting taped to the back of the board.

4 Leave the fabric in the sun until it is completely dry. Remove the objects and heat set the printed fabric.

Paper stencils will not print as perfectly as plastic stencils because wet paper warps and lets the sun underneath—but sometimes perfect is not the effect we're going for. This piece was printed twice—once with a paper stencil and once with a plastic stencil.

A cut-out letter page meant for scrapbooking makes a perfect resist. Search hardware and craft stores for items that will block the sun in interesting ways.

Cheesecloth makes beautiful patterns when draped and sun printed. When the cheesecloth absorbs enough paint to look good all by itself, use it for collage.

Kid Friendly

Diluted Textile Color by Jacquard and Setacolor Transparent paint by Pebeo also work well for sun printing. The paints are non-toxic and safe for kids to use. Have your children create a fun summer t-shirt or tote bag with sun printing

Monoprinting

Monoprinting is an old technique used for printing onto paper. Today's fabric artists love the process because they can paint on a surface for an indefinite time, and once the desired look is achieved, print it onto fabric.

Monoprinting allows artists to create multiple prints from one paint setup. I often get a second print, which I usually like better than the first! Even a third print is sometimes possible as you'll see from the samples below. Any paint that stays put on a glass or plastic surface will work. I use Lumiere, Setacolor, and Neopaque. If you really like serendipitous results, spray water onto the paint. Old masters would be shocked at such a loose way of printing, but we are having WAY more fun!

"Mist in the Garden" by Shelli Ricci. Shelli used drops of paint, water, and Pearl Ex powder to create this delightful little piece. The lines were formed by drawing a palette knife through puddles of paint. Shelli used a related piece to make a fabric postcard with thread painting.

Monoprinting Basics

1 Add open acrylic medium (available at art supply stores) to fabric paint to keep paint from drying on the glass or plastic surface. The medium lends a slightly plastic feel to the paint when dry, but allows you to move the paint around for as long as you like before pulling a print.

2 Cover the edges of glass sheet with masking tape to protect your hands, or use a piece of acrylic or template plastic.

3 Use a sponge brush to apply paint onto glass or plastic surface.

4 To pull a print, drop fabric face down on painted print plate and rub back of fabric with your hands; clean paint from your hands as you go. (For the pictured project, Copper Pearl Ex powdered pigment was smeared onto a plastic surface and then blue paint was sponge-brushed over the pigment. The first print was pulled off, and then the plate was sprayed with water and a second print was pulled.)

5 Carefully pull the fabric off the plate and set aside to dry. Heat set the fabric to make the printed design permanent.

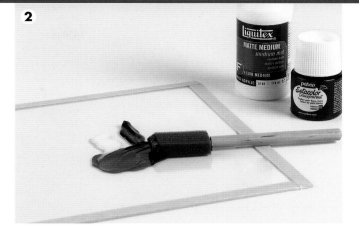

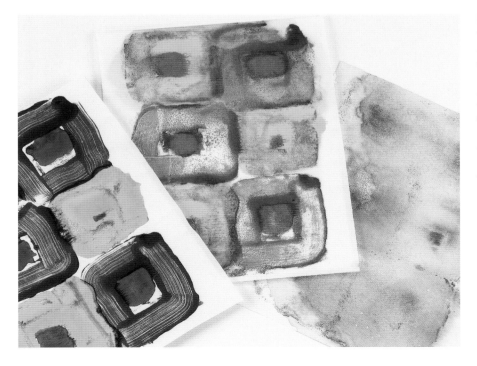

For this trio of prints, paint was applied to the plate with a sponge brush; the paint was wet enough to allow blue and yellow to mix and create green highlights. The second print was made by spraying water on the remaining paint, which created interesting spots and bleeding. For the third print, the plate was sprinkled with powdered Pearl Ex and sprayed heavily with water, which caused colors to lighten and run together and make more green, purple, and orange from the setup's original three primaries.

Paint was applied to the print plate with a sponge and then a foam stamp was used to remove paint. Wipe the stamp onto a paper towel each time you remove paint from the plate. Or, wipe the stamp onto another piece of fabric to start your next project.

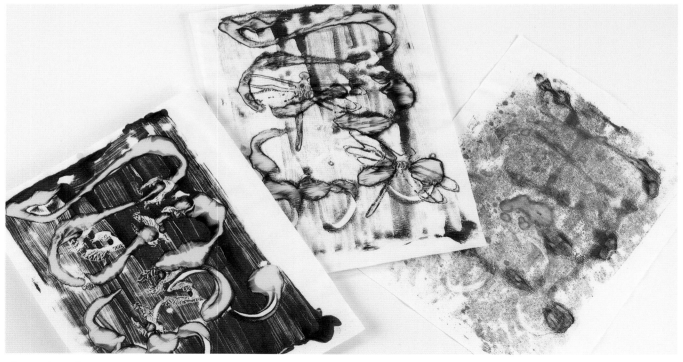

The print plate was painted blue with a sponge brush and then yellow paint was poured on. A sponge stamp and a cotton swab were used to remove some paint. The first print was pulled, which forced the blue and yellow to mix. The second print was done on the fabric used to wipe off the stamp from the previous step. The third print, where the remaining paint was sprayed with water, is pastel blue with interesting green markings.

A purse by Tina Hughes illustrates a great use of color and the monoprinting technique done with a stamp.

Experiment

Clearly this chapter illustrates the "what if" method of experimenting and playing with an old technique. Invite a friend over to bounce monoprinting ideas around. It will be a very entertaining afternoon that's likely to produce collections of new fabric pieces, perfect for your next sewing or collage project.

Silk scarves
by Nancy Mambi

Soy Wax Batik

Batik is a way of resisting paint or dye that has been done in many cultures for a very long time. The technique can be very complex, with dozens of processes applied to the fabric by different artisans. We benefit from these artists' mastery when we buy batiks to make clothing or quilts. Artists in Indonesia, Malaysia, and parts of Africa specialize in making and exporting gorgeous batik fabrics.

The original batik process involves waxing cotton or rayon fabrics in patterns; the wax is often applied with carefully handcrafted metal devices dipped in hot wax and printed onto the fabric hundreds of times. At other times, the wax is applied with a tjanting tool, which is a tiny well at the end of a handle that has a pipe coming out the end to deliver wax to the fabric. After the wax hardens, the fabric is dyed in large vats, rewaxed, and dyed again in a different color. Wherever wax is applied, the color is resisted so the fabric stays the original or previously dyed color. The wax is removed by boiling the fabric or by ironing out most of the wax and then dry-cleaning the fabric.

With the arrival of soy wax, batik became easier for artists who want to try this fascinating technique. Soy wax does not give off noxious fumes, is used at a much lower temperature so is safer to use, can be cleaned up with hot tap water and soap, and, when released, doesn't hurt plumbing. Soy wax readily releases from fabric when the color is completed and the fabric is ironed between paper towels and soaked in hot soapy water. An extra benefit is that soy wax is made from soy beans, not petroleum! Dharma carries soy wax, and you can also buy candle wax made for pillar candles (but not for container candles; the wax is softer).

To create patterns, place chicken wire, sink liners, textured shelf liners, and other textured items under the fabric and apply wax to the top of the fabric. Use brushes, tjanting tools, and kitchen utensils to apply wax to the top of the fabric. Hot wax must penetrate the fabric to act as a resist so check the back of the fabric while you are working. If necessary, apply wax to the back side of the patterns you've made on the front. If the wax starts to smoke, it is too hot and the heat should be turned down to prevent a fire. After applying the wax, set fabric aside to harden and then color it at any time. Do not lay your waxed pieces in the sun as the wax will re-melt and you will lose your pattern, a lesson I learned through personal experience!

YOU WILL NEED

- soy wax flakes (see resources)
- electric frying pan
- bristle brushes, kitchen utensils, tjanting tools, flat metal objects with handles, metal scrubbers with handles, carved wooden blocks, textured shelf liner, kitchen sink liners, and flat textured items that will resist heat
- oilcloth table cloth
- scraper or credit card
- PFD fabric, black and white
- dye, soda ash
- Dye-na-Flow fabric paint by Jacquard (see resources)
- diluted bleach in spray bottle
- Anti-Chlor bleach neutralizer (see resources)
- Discharge Paste by Jacquard (see resources)
- small plastic containers with covers or plastic bags
- 1" (2.5 cm) sponge brushes
- Paper towels for ironing off wax

Soy Wax Batik Basics

1 Place wax flakes in an electric frying pan and set the temperature dial to about 140° F (60° C).

2 Cover your work surface with an oilcloth table cloth—the oilcloth makes it easy to scrape off dripped wax with a credit card and put wax back into pan.

3 Place various objects in the pan of melted wax and let them heat up. Pull an object from wax, let excess wax drip back

into the pan, and print the hot wax onto the fabric, checking to make sure wax shows on back of fabric. If it doesn't show, turn up the frying pan's temperature a bit.

4 Or, place a dimensional item beneath the waxed fabric and lightly brush the top of the fabric to pick up the texture or pattern of the item below. Put the waxed fabric aside to harden.

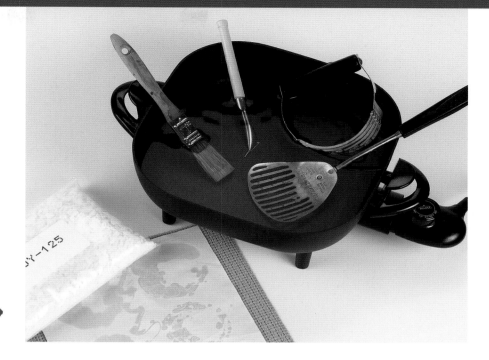

5 Mix a small amount of dye (see dyeing chapter) and add soda ash dissolved in water. Place waxed white fabric in a baggie or small plastic container.

6 Pour the dye over the fabric and push the fabric down with gloved hands. Cover the container or close the baggie and let fabric stand for four or more hours in a warm room.

7 Pour off the dye and wash the fabric in hot tap water and soap to remove excess dye and wax. The areas that were waxed will remain white, with interesting crackles.

Handling Tools

Let your batik tools harden in the wax-filled frying pan and you'll know exactly where to find them when it's time for your next project. When carrying wax-loaded tools from the frying pan to the fabric, hold a small board or piece of cardboard under the tools to catch drips.

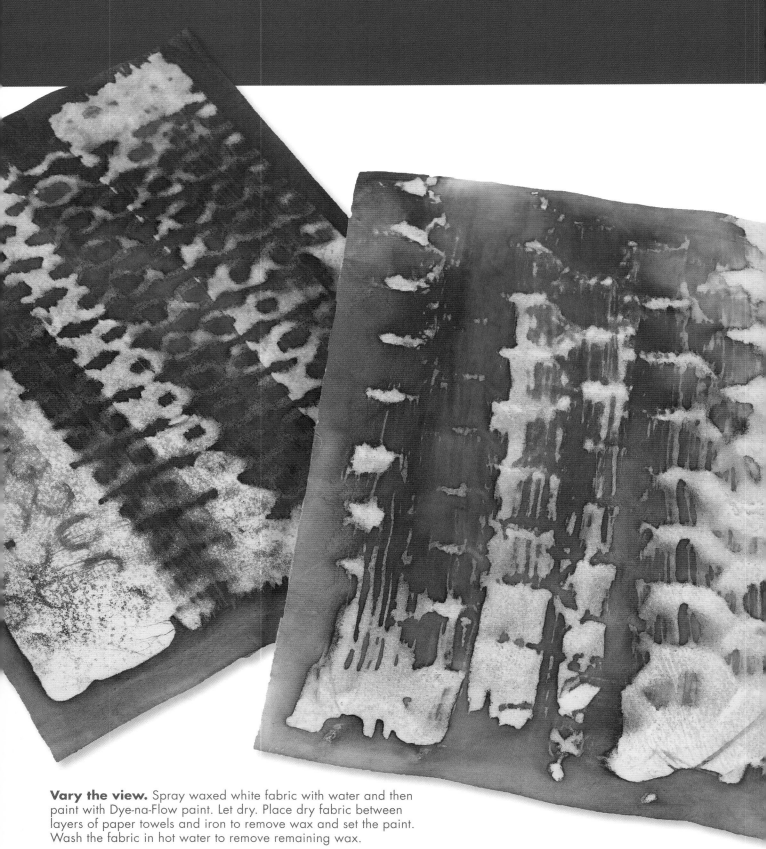

Vary the view. Spray waxed white fabric with water and then paint with Dye-na-Flow paint. Let dry. Place dry fabric between layers of paper towels and iron to remove wax and set the paint. Wash the fabric in hot water to remove remaining wax.

Discharge Batik

1 Wax black fabric, let wax harden, and then paint the surface with discharge paste.

2 Let the fabric partially dry and then place it between paper towels on the ironing board. Iron to remove the wax and activate the discharge paste. You may need to iron the fabric without the paper towels to fully activate the discharge paste. Look at the back of the fabric to see if it is prettier than the front.

3 Wash the fabric to remove all the wax and paste.

Vary the view. Spray waxed black fabric with a half and half mix of bleach and water. Watch until the desired color change is reached. Immediately dunk fabric in hot soapy water to remove the wax and bleach. Soak in Anti-Chlor to neutralize the bleach (page 23).

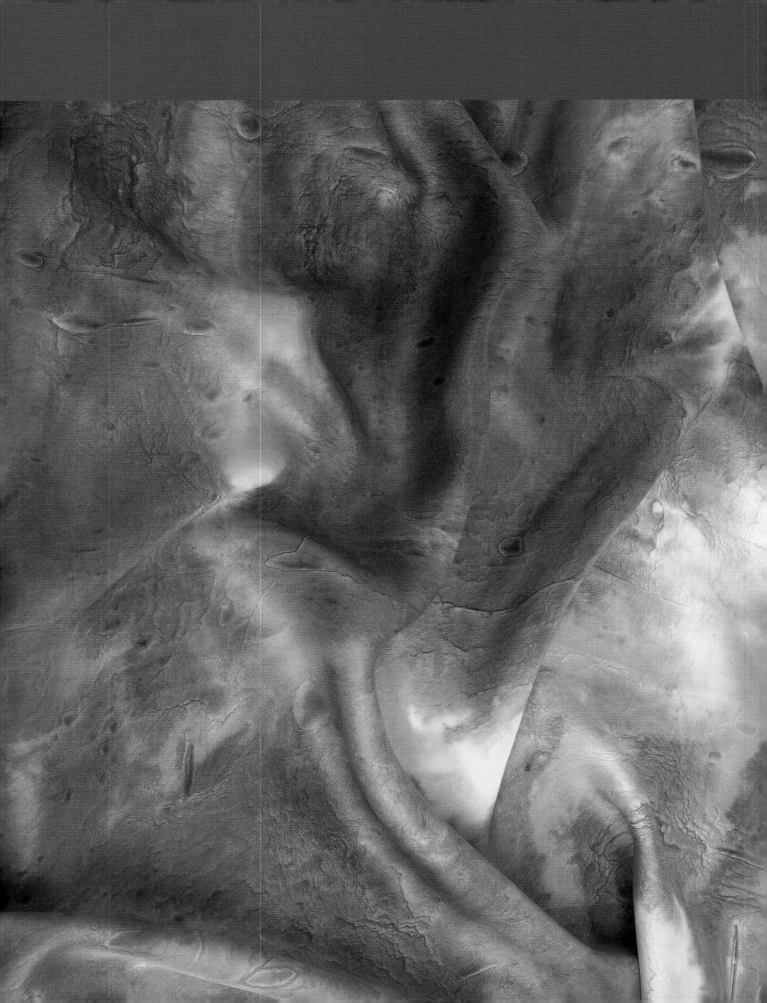

Dyeing

Dyeing your own fabric brings a real sense of satisfaction because every part of the artistic process is your own. Once you have mastered the art of dyeing, you can make fabric any color and pattern you choose, while ensuring that there will be no other art piece quite like yours. Dyeing involves much more time and preparation than painting on fabric but produces a rich saturated look and maintains the "hand" of the fabric.

After being dyed, both sides of the fabric will be essentially the same and the patterning, which is determined by the amount of agitation applied during the dyeing process, can vary from solid color to heavily textured to suede-like. Patterns can also be introduced with mechanical resists like folding, tying, and clamping (see tie-dyeing chapter) or chemical resists like wax (see batik chapter). Commercial fabrics can be over-dyed to make them better blend with your needs, while black and white fabrics can be given any background color you choose. Even finished quilts can be dyed to make their colors and patterns appear more unified or to give them a monochromatic scheme.

There are different kinds of dyes (even crayons and markers that contain dye are available) but most people use Procion MX fiber reactive dyes for large pieces of fabric. They are permanent on natural fibers, such as cotton, linen, silk, and rayon, and, when an acid like vinegar is added, can be used on wool. Colors will dye differently on

YOU WILL NEED

- Procion MX series dye (see resources)
- soda ash dye activator (see resources)
- Synthrapol detergent (see resources)
- non-iodized salt
- Pro Print Paste SH for thickening dye (see resources)
- urea (for direct dyeing) (see resources)
- PFD fabric (see resources)
- two buckets or wash basins for immersion dyeing
- long-handled spoons for stirring dye
- measuring cups and spoons
- small containers for mixing and storing dye

- heavy duty one-gallon plastic zipper bags for low-immersion dyeing
- rubber gloves
- dust mask
- apron
- cardboard box for measuring dye
- basin for baggies
- old towels
- screens, stamps, and stencils for direct dyeing
- plastic sheeting
- whisk or blender to mix thickener

silk and wool fabrics (which are protein fiber) than they will on cellulose fibers, such as cotton, linen, and rayon. Dyes used for synthetic fabrics are highly toxic and not practical for home use. Natural dyes are safe but the mordants needed to set them are not, so proceed with caution if pursuing that route.

Procion dyes react chemically with fabric fibers through the addition of soda ash to the process and do not have to be heat set or steamed like some other dyes. The only other ingredients needed are urea for direct applications (to make water wetter); Synthrapol for washing out excess dye after rinsing; print paste to thicken dye for direct applications; and salt. Every instructor or book provides slightly different information on "the only" way to dye so it is important to do your own testing. Different communities have different types of water,

humidity levels, and temperature conditions so you may have to adjust dyes by adding water softeners or other chemicals. When dyeing, work in a warm location away from food, pets, and children. Although the dyes and chemicals are fairly safe, keep clearly marked dyeing equipment and dyes in a designated area and never use the same utensils for food prep and dyeing.

Immersion dyeing means that fabric is completely submerged in dye; depending on how much the fabric is moved, color will be more uniform and only one color is achieved. Immersion dyeing can be used to produce gradations—a value range from light to dark—which can be used to make very dramatic pieces with simple sewing. Low-immersion dyeing is often used to produce more mottling on the fabric. Baggies or small containers are used and the fabric is scrunched to promote color

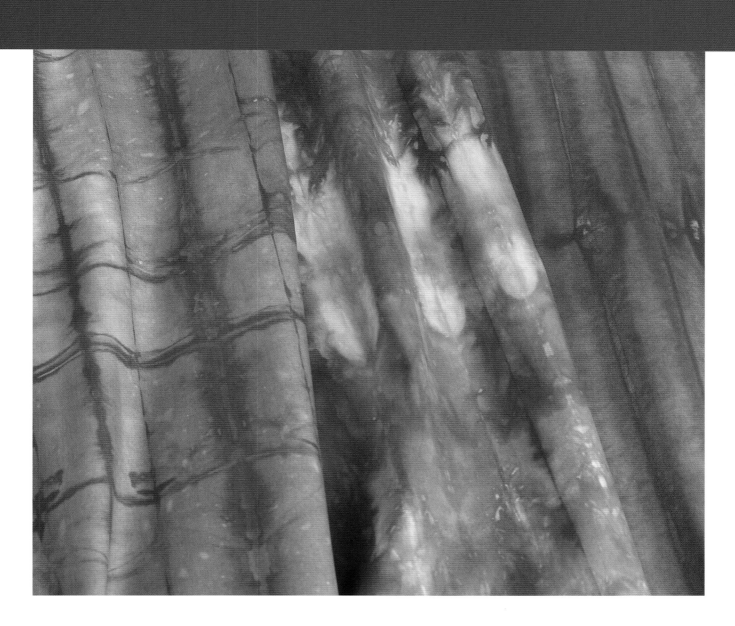

value differences and visual texture. Although you can use several colors on a single piece of fabric, take care not to create "mud" colors by mixing too many colors or using opposites on the color wheel.

Keep records of the dyes used to create a project so you can later replicate a favorite color. It isn't necessary to buy a lot of different colors of dye. You can mix any color using primary colors and black, but you may want several dyes in different yellows, reds, and blues. When mixed with water, Procion dyes keep for some time in the refrigerator, but once soda ash is added they will be exhausted in a few hours. Make up dye concentrates, store them, and add more water when

you're ready to use them. Although it is common to soda ash the fabric before dyeing it, some dyers will not add soda ash to the process until after the fabric has soaked in dye for several hours.

Again, there are many variables that affect the dyeing process. Some people have found baggies of fabric that have been soaking for months, and the fabrics are none the worse for wear! When I started dyeing classes in the 1980s, no mottling was allowed and one little spot of lighter value was considered a failure. Now, dyeing is a whole lot more fun, and the fabric is more interesting to use. Just be sure to actually use it, instead of storing it in a drawer. You can always dye more fabric!

Preparing Dye

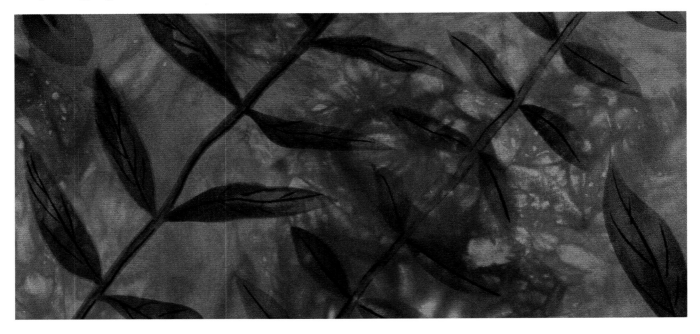

1 Before preparing dye concentrate, put on rubber gloves and a dust mask.

2 Measure dye into a cup (250 mL) of warm water, being careful not to spill powder or release dust into the air. Use one to two tablespoons (37.5 mL) of dye, depending on the intensity of color you want.

3 Mix dye until it is dissolved—some colors will take longer to dissolve than others. After the dye is dissolved, remove your mask. This concentrate can be kept for a few weeks in the refrigerator—be sure to mark it clearly (it's best to have a small refrigerator in your studio just for dye).

Tip

Set a cardboard box on its side and line the bottom side with wet paper towels. Set the measuring cup of water in the box and measure the dye powder inside. The loose dye powder will be caught by the box instead of flying into the air. Immediately close the cover on the jar of dye.

Full Immersion Dyeing

1 Wearing a dust mask, mix ¼ cup (60 mL) of soda ash into one cup (250 mL) of very hot water and add to one gallon (3.8 L) of cool water.

2 Place PFD fabric in the soda ash solution and soak at least 15 minutes. The soda ash will set the dye permanently.

3 Fill a second bucket with one gallon (3.8 L) of lukewarm water and one cup (250 mL) of non-iodized salt. Pour in dye concentrate according to the intensity of color desired and mix thoroughly.

4 Place the wet fabric (wring it out a little) into the dye water, submerging it quickly and stirring to remove air bubbles and tight wrinkles. Soak the fabric for four hours or more (called "batching"), stirring occasionally for more even color.

5 Remove the fabric from the bucket and rinse in warm water and then hot water until most of the excess dye is removed. Machine-wash in hot water and Synthrapol. Dry until damp and then iron.

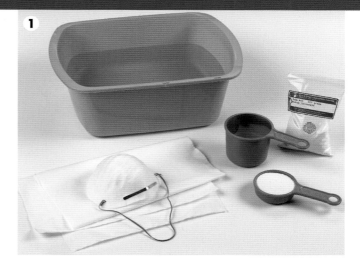

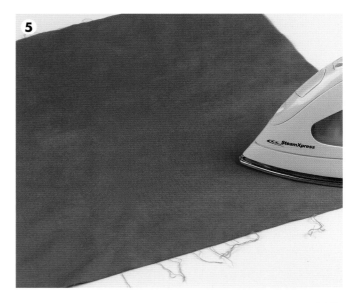

Low Immersion Dyeing

1 For low-immersion dyeing, soak fat quarters (18" x 22" [45.5 x 56 cm]) of fabric in the soda ash solution as before. Put each of the wet pieces into a separate one gallon bag, scrunched evenly.

2 Add ¼ cup (60 mL) salt to the dye concentrate and then add water according to the intensity of color desired. (Try making gradations by pouring greater and greater amounts of concentrate into eight one-cup (250 mL) measures and then filling to the one-cup (250 mL) level with water.)

3 Pour one cup (250 mL) of dye over each fabric. Seal the bags, squeeze the bags to make sure the dye permeates the fabric, and place them in the wash basin to "batch". If you like less mottling, squeeze the bags periodically.

4 After four to twenty-four hours, process as in step 5 for batch dyeing. These fabrics will have much more visual texture because of the small amount of water, less agitation, and the scrunching.

Choosing Fabric

Unbleached muslin for dyeing can be used but its cream color will affect the final results. Sheeting works well but will give softer detail than pima cotton, which is finely woven and shows crinkling better, but is harder to stitch and more expensive. Broadcloth is lightweight and sews as easily as muslin without the color influence. Always test fabrics not marked PFD (prepared-for-dyeing). Any finishes or synthetic content will affect how the dye is absorbed.

Direct Application Dyeing

1 For direct application dyeing, mix three cups of hot water with ¾ cup (177 mL) of salt and ⅓ cup (79 mL) of urea (this is called chemical water).

2 Pour a small amount into a cup and add dye concentrate to get the color value you want.

3 Mix print paste by slowly adding 2 tablespoons (30 mL) to a cup (250 mL) of water, stirring constantly. When the print paste is smooth, (you may want to mix it the day before), mix it with dye to make the consistency you need for the technique you will be using—stamping, screen printing, or stenciling.

4 Apply the thickened dye to dry soda-ash soaked fabric as instructed in the chapters detailing the technique you are using.

5 After printing, cover face of fabric with plastic to keep fabric layers separated, roll up the fabric, seal, and let batch for 24 hours in a warm place before rinsing and washing.

Here are eight fat quarters, each with a different look. The dyeing for each fabric began with a single cup of dye concentrate— one part black and five parts terra cotta (the bright orange color used in full-immersion dying, page 135). The one cup (250 mL) of concentrate was divided among eight plastic cups, with less dye poured into each successive cup. From those two colors came taupe, green, dark red, brown, and fascinating patterns. The baggies were not disturbed after the initial agitation, causing extreme value variations.

You may like more subtle markings, which are easy to achieve by manipulating the bags during batching. These color-gradation samples, dyed by Susan Antell, show more controlled mottling. Dyeing is not something that you'll perfect in one session, but it is a process that will fascinate you for months to come.

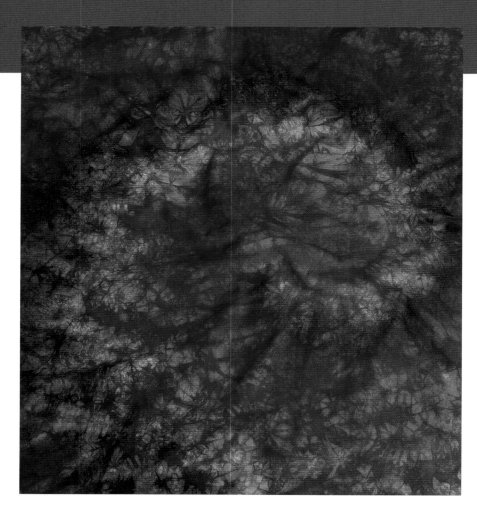

Fabric is scrunched and spiraled, then dyed in rainbow colors. By Joy Press.

The amount of scrunching will affect the distribution of color in low immersion dying.

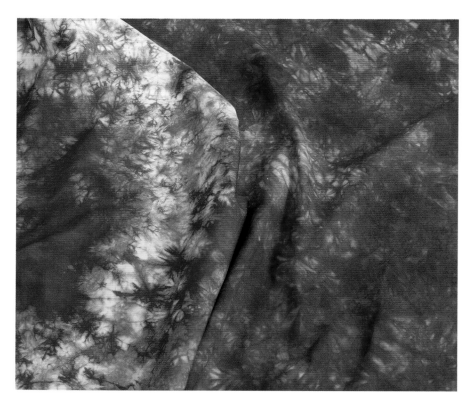

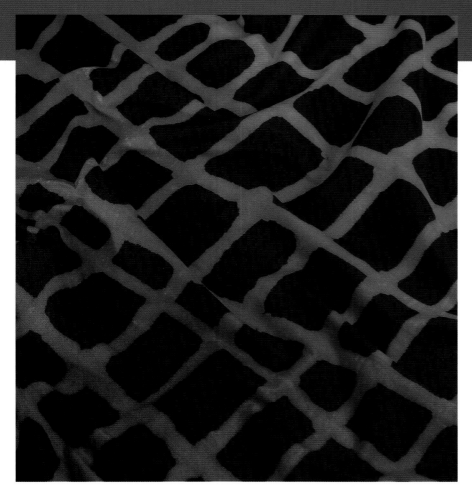

Black cotton was discharged first and then dyed again. By Diane Bartels.

Scrunching the fabric into a flat container like a plastic sweater box will allow you to pour dye on specific areas.

Tie-Dyeing

This technique's name brings to mind bright primary colors dyed into a swirl on t-shirts. Tie-dye offers so many more options and includes ancient Japanese techniques called shibori, wonderful folded designs, and resisted designs achieved with clamps and stitching.

Tie-dye technique is related to direct dyeing but does not involve thickening dyes. Instead, dye is applied with a squeeze bottle, then the fabric is batched in a plastic bag. You can also do these techniques with Dye-na-Flow paint, since color is directly applied in the same ways. If you're using paint, do not soak fabric in soda ash and remember to heat set the fabric after the paint dries.

YOU WILL NEED

- PFD fabrics, such as cotton, silk, rayon, or linen

- Procion MX dye (see resources)

- soda ash (see resources)

- urea (see resources)

- salt

- measuring cups and spoons

- rubber gloves

- dust mask

- containers for mixing dye

- squeeze bottles

- rubber bands

- strong thread

- sewing needle with large eye

- C-clamp

- Plexiglas, metal, or wood squares or circles

- PVC pipe

- string or cord

- plastic baggies

- Synthrapol detergent (see resources)

Tie-Dye Basics

1 Cut fabrics into pieces. Soak pieces in a solution of one gallon (3.8 L) water and ¼ cup (60 mL) of soda ash (see page 135). Prepare dye with concentrate, urea, and salt (see page 135).

2 Pour dye into a squeeze bottle. For the first sample, wring out a piece of fabric, grab its center, and rubber band tightly in three places. Squeeze dye into the folds and put the fabric in a plastic bag to batch for 24 hours.

3 Cut and remove the rubber bands; rinse and wash fabric (see page 135).

Vary the view #1. Lay a piece of soda-ash-soaked fabric on the table. Place a cord diagonally across the fabric. Fold the fabric in half over the cord; twirl the fabric in the air until it wraps around the cord; scrunch the fabric on the cord; and tie a knot in the cord. Squeeze dye into the folds, place in a bag, and batch 24 hours. Process as above.

Vary the view #2. Wrap a piece of soda ash soaked fabric loosely around a piece of PVC pipe, and then scrunch it together. Squeeze dye over the fabric, getting it into the folds. Put the pipe into a bag and batch for 24 hours. Process as above. (For a different dyed look, wrap the fabric diagonally around the pipe.)

Vary the view #3. Lay a piece of soda-ash-soaked fabric on the table and place your thumb and index finger in the center. With your other hand, spiral the fabric around the center. Put the fabric roll in a container that will hold fabric's shape, squeeze the dye onto the fabric, and cover tightly for 24 hours. Process as above.

Vary the view #4. Pull up and wrap tiny portions of soda-ash-soaked fabric piece with strong thread and tie off. Place a bead or marble in the bubble-like pocket to create more perfect circles. Squeeze dye onto the fabric, place fabric in a plastic bag for 24 hours, and process as above.

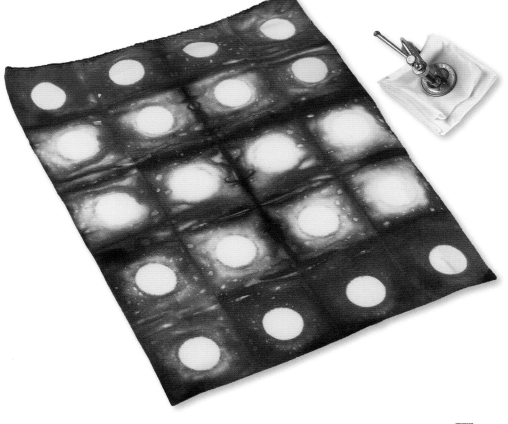

Vary the view #5. Accordion-pleat ash-soaked fabric. With the squeeze bottle, squirt dye down each side of pleats. Roll the pleated fabric and place it in a plastic bag for 24 hours. (Or, diagonally pleat fabric and roll it before applying dye.) Rinse and wash.

Vary the view #6. Accordion-pleat soaked fabric, and then accordion fold it again in the other direction, so that you have a square. Clamp matching pieces of wood, plastic, or metal on each side to make a fabric sandwich and tighten the clamp, which will act as a resist to the dye. Squeeze dye on exposed fabric, place in a plastic bag for 24 hours, and process as above.

Line-dry a piece of soda-ash-soaked fabric. Hand stitch several lines of running stitches into the fabric using heavy thread. Stitch the single layer or make pleats and stitch near the folds. Gather up the threads and tie off. Squeeze dye onto the fabric, place in a plastic bag for 24 hours, cut and remove the threads, and process as above.

Results Vary

● ●

Just like any dyeing process, different artists use different formulas and techniques, so test every step of the dyeing process and get dyeing tips from other dyers in your area. Even the amount of chlorine in your water can affect dyeing, as will humidity, temperature, and hardness of water.

● ●

STITCHING, WEAVING, AND FELTING

Sewing is an important pastime for millions of women and men. Being creative brings a real sense of accomplishment, and being able to sew home decorating items, clothes, and gifts saves money, while providing items that sometimes far surpass the appeal of readymade things.

This section explains sewing basics, such as the principles of appliqué and machine quilting, how to create your own fabrics, and ways to alter and manipulate fabrics to make exciting new textures. There are few extra supplies required, so have fun using your creative stash, whether it is fabric, thread, or wool and silk fibers.

Silk Fusion

This is a wonderful way to make fabric out of silk roving, which is soft and luxurious and comes in gorgeous hand-dyed colors. The resulting fusion can be extremely sheer or very firm and opaque.

Use the fused fabric for purses, book covers, wall pieces, neck pieces, and vessels. Experiment with textile mediums you have on hand (choose mediums that won't make the fusion sticky) or use acrylic medium for a stiffer product. Add in ribbons, skeleton leaves, Angelina fiber, or other embellishments as you layer the silk; be sure the added elements stand up to moisture. Or, decorate the fusion after it dries.

YOU WILL NEED

- tulle or netting, approximately a 10" x 14" (25.5 x 35.5 cm) piece

- silk roving (also try viscose roving)

- embellishments, decorative threads, or beads (optional)

- shampoo without conditioner

- bristle paint brush

- textile medium (Pebeo or Jacquard brands recommended)

- fluid acrylic medium

- Misty Fuse adhesive web

- Bo-Nash Bonding Agent (granulated adhesive)

- fabric for front, back, and binding (finished piece measures about 13" x 18" [33 x 44.5 cm])

- small piece of fusible batting

- cooking parchment

Fusion Basics

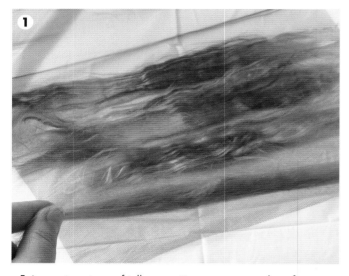

1 Lay out a piece of tulle or netting on your work surface. Pull small amounts of silk fiber from the hank of roving and lay them parallel to each other on half of the tulle in a thin and even layer. For the nicest look, never cut the silk roving. Hold your hands about 8" (20.3 cm) apart on the hank of roving and pull it apart.

2 Lay additional fibers crosswise on top of the first layer. Lay a third layer of fibers in the direction of the first layer. Check for thin spots in the layers and fill in, if necessary.

3 Lay silk or skeleton leaves, ribbons, or other decorative elements on top of the third layer of fibers. Cover them with wisps of fibers to hold them in place. Fold the other half of the tulle over the top of the layered silk fibers and embellishments.

4 Dissolve about ½ teaspoon (2.5 mL) of shampoo into 2 cups (0.5 L) of water. Brush the solution on the tulle until all layers are thoroughly saturated. Blot out as much water as possible with paper towels. Coat both sides of the tulle with full-strength textile medium. Let the fusion dry on a screen or piece of plastic mesh and then peel it off the tulle.

Make Stitched Art

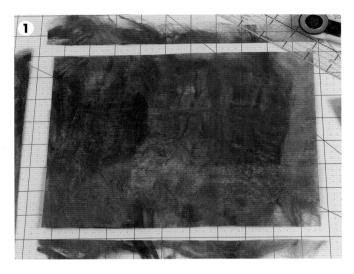

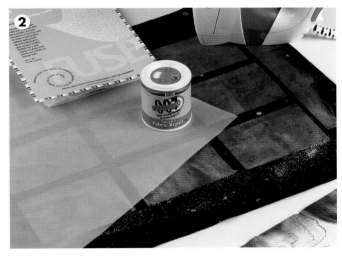

1 Use the fusion to make a small stitched wall piece by cutting off irregular edges to create a square or rectangle. Save cut off edges for borders. Measure sides of square or rectangle and add 6" (15.2 cm) to each measurement. Cut a piece of contrasting fabric to that measurement and iron fusible batting to the back, using a steam iron.

2 Lay the silk fusion wrong side up on a piece of cooking parchment placed on an ironing board. Cover it with a piece of Misty Fuse adhesive web and place another piece of cooking parchment over the top. Press with a dry iron.

3 Cut the silk fusion into nine equal pieces and arrange on the fabric piece. Cover with cooking parchment and iron silk into place. Sprinkle granulated adhesive in the border areas and arrange the trimmed fusion pieces on top. Brush or blow away the excess granules, cover with parchment, and iron.

4 Trim the fabric to the desired size and cut a piece of fabric 2" (5 cm) larger all the way around for the backing and fuse it to the back of the batting. Stitch around the edges of the fusion sections, adding decorative threads, ribbons, or other embellishments.

5 Trim the backing to 1" (2.5 cm) extra around the edges, press under ½" (1.3 cm), and bring the folded edge to the front. Sew along the fold, folding in the corners, to make a binding.

6 Add a casing for hanging to the back, or mount fusion on a stretched canvas that is painted to match.

Make a Purse

1 Make a silk purse (not out of sow's ear but from silk roving) from a 9" x 14" (23 x 35.5 cm) piece of fusion, with different colors on each side. (Most skeins of hand-dyed roving have several colors in them.) Place the drying fusion on something that allows air to circulate around both sides to avoid a plastic look on one side. When the fusion is totally dry, take off the netting and straighten the sides.

2 Cut one end (which will be the edge of flap) with a decorative edge, such as zigzags, scallops, or waves, or leave one end with a soft edge.

3 Sew with decorative thread all over the fusion and very close to both ends.

4 Fold up the bottom edge about one third of the length (or a little more if needed) and sew up both sides to make a pocket; extend the stitching to the top edge to reinforce it.

5 Press the decorative end down over the pocket to make a flap. Sew Velcro on flap and pocket edges and decorate flap with a button.

6 Add a ribbon strap by sewing it to the back, just below the fold of the flap.

Make a Bowl

1 To make a silk paper bowl, drape silk roving in alternating directions over a pottery bowl. Cover with netting, wet and blot the construction, and coat with acrylic medium.

2 Remove the netting while the fusion is wet. Add more medium to silk fusion so it saturates the roving, and carefully smooth out the silk before letting it dry thoroughly.

3 Remove the dry silk from the pottery bowl. Embellish as desired. Remember to decorate the inside as well as the outside of finished bowl.

Sticking

If nylon netting sticks to the silk fusion, switch to another medium, reduce the amount of medium used, or use coarser netting.

Cut Fabric Weaving

Make an exciting background for a small wall hanging or front panels for a unique vest or jacket by weaving randomly cut fabric strips together to make a new textile. By ironing fusible web to the back of two fabrics, you will avoid any raveling and the weaving will be easy to control while you add decorative stitching or other embellishments.

Choosing a fabric with a printed gradation will lend an exciting element with no added work; using a batik for the other fabric adds another artistic touch because the colors will vary across the weaving's surface.

Cut Fabric Weaving Basics

1 Following manufacturer's directions, iron fusible web, such as Wonder-Under, to the back of both fabrics. Remove the web's paper backing and save for later use as a press sheet.

2 Lay the two fabrics separately on a cutting mat. Use a rotary cutter to cut wavy horizontal and vertical lines, spaced about 1½" (4 cm) apart, freehand across the pieces. Keep the strips in the order in which they were cut.

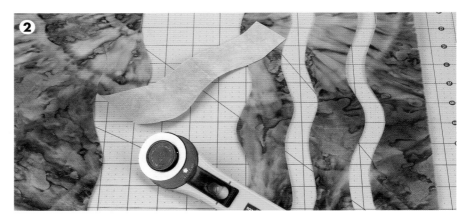

3 Place release paper from the fusible web on an ironing board. Place the vertically cut set of strips on the release paper in order and tape the ends to the ironing board with masking tape.

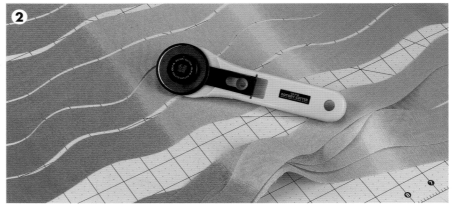

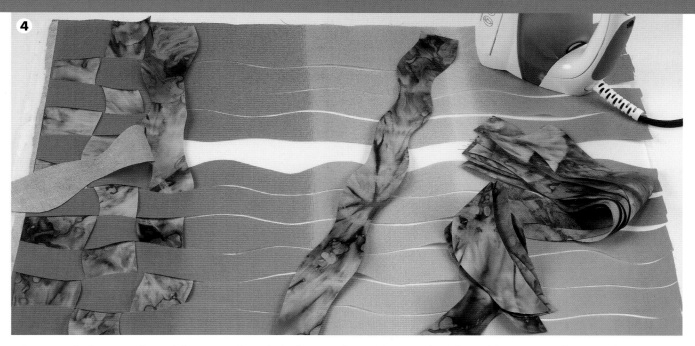

4 Weave the horizontally cut fabric strips through the first set of strips, keeping the edges of the strips as close together as possible. Note: It's easiest to weave in a new strip by lifting every other vertical strip and laying it back over the taped edge. Then place the horizontal strip in place and flop the vertical strips back into place. For the next row, lay alternating verticals over the taped edge and place the horizontal strip in place.

5 When weaving is complete, dry iron over the top of the weaving to tack it together. Carefully move the weaving from the paper onto a piece of batting. Thoroughly steam-iron stacked pieces.

6 With the backing steamed to the other side of the batting, stitch down the centers of the strips, over the cut edges, or stitch an allover pattern across the whole piece. Add appliqués, beads, or other embellishments. Trim and bind the edges or cut into a garment section.

From each fabric, cut straighter strips that are narrower in the middle and wider at the edges. Draw chalk lines on the fabric to ensure strips come out right. Or, draw lines on large pieces of tracing paper and pin to the fabrics to use as cutting guides. Weave the strips as above and embellish. This example is foiled using a granulated adhesive for the glue.

Choose a fabric that has a large scene or floral design that will show up in the weaving. As you quilt the weaving, outline the hidden motifs with stitch lines in high contrast thread.

Fusing

When using Wonder-Under or other paper-backed fusible webs, iron web onto the back of the fabric and let cool before peeling off release paper. When arranging the backed pieces of fabric onto batting or a background, tack in place with a dry iron. When satisfied with the arrangement, steam the pieces into place permanently.

Chenille

Chenille is a very textured and luxurious fabric that you make with multiple layers of fabric. You can use muslin, plaids, stripes, or solids that have been languishing in your stash because only the outer two layers will show. Or, splurge on wonderful rayon batiks, hand-dyeds, or even flannel fabrics.

The key considerations when choosing fabrics for chenille are that the front and back will be the same when they fray and that you will still have saturated color (unless you can use the lighter back color as an asset). Test batiks because they don't ravel easily. The bottom layer will show through the cut channels so make sure it complements the top layer.
The other essential step in successfully making chenille is to make a test sample of fabric combinations you are considering. Some fabrics will not fray, no matter what you do. You may want to arrange the same layers in different ways to see how layering affects the look. Remember to always stitch at a 45-degree angle to the straight of grain to maximize texture.

YOU WILL NEED

- eight-step bundle of hand-dyed colors in a light to dark gradation (see resources)
- thread
- sewing machine
- scissors
- four fabrics: print, plaid, and two solids
- ½ yd (0.5 m) white fabric
- eighteen 3" (7.5 cm) squares of colored fabric

Chenille Basics

1 Layer a hand-dyed muslin gradation, using seven values of the same color and cut a pile of 8" (20.5 cm) squares.

2 Draw a line—from corner to corner on the square—on the top fabric and pin the layers together.

3 Using a walking foot on the sewing machine, stitch over the marked line. Using the walking foot edge as a guide, stitch ⅜" (.95 cm) to ½"(1.3 cm) away from the first line. Continue to stitch lines, switching the direction of stitching each time so the top layer doesn't shift.

4 Cut through the top six layers of fabric with a sharp scissors, being careful not to cut through the bottom layer.

5 At the sink, wet the fabric piece and rub it between your hands to start the fraying. Toss the piece in the dryer with a towel and dry thoroughly. (For large projects, use the washing machine on a short cycle to start the fraying.) Keep notes on each test piece so you know which fabrics you used. You can even use thin cotton batting that you've dyed as one of the layers.

To test the effect of a fabric's position within the stack, cut four pieces of fabric, one large print, one yarn-dyed plaid, and two plain fabrics. In the first sample, place the plaid directly under the top layer so the two solids are on the bottom. In the second, place the two solids in the middle, making the plaid the back layer. In the first sample, the leaves stand out a little less but the black background is more interesting with the plaid influencing its appearance. In the second sample, the plaid is mostly hidden by the top three layers, but if the piece was used in a garment it could be very interesting as the body moved and revealed the garment's inside layer.

Do you want a diffused look or more color? Cut eight 9" (23 cm) squares of white fabric and eighteen 3" (7.5 cm) squares of colored fabric. Place nine colored squares on top of three layers of white fabric. Cover with another piece of white fabric. For a second sample, cover four layers of white fabric with the remaining colored squares. Stitch and cut both samples; then, rinse, and dry. Instead of using squares of color, cut out images or appliqué shapes and leave white spaces between them. You'll find that the sample with a layer of white over the colors will look much softer than the color-over-white sample.

Here's another idea.
Lee Bradford, maker of this sophisticated and very wearable vest, used several layers of hand-dyed rayon and selectively cut between the stitching lines to chenille part of the piece and showcase the fabric on the other part.

Fray More

If you want a little more fraying after the chenille piece is dry, go over it with a suede brush.

Quilted Effects

Quilting secures three layers—top, batting, and backing—together. Stitching can be very decorative or simply functional and hidden in patchwork seam lines. Today hundreds of threads—cotton, silk, rayon, metallic, variegated, invisible, and polyester—allow quilters to customize any project's quilting.

Machine quilting can be done on the simplest sewing machine or on a very complicated computerized longarm machine. The mechanics of the two kinds of machines are different; the domestic machine requires movement of the quilt under the needle and the longarm moves the machine over stationary quilt layers. No matter which machine is used, the final effect is the same. A quilt doesn't look finished until the quilting is complete, no matter how beautiful the appliqué or piecing.

YOU WILL NEED

- cotton fabrics for fronts and backs
- cotton or cotton/polyester batting
- thread
- walking foot
- darning foot
- sewing machine
- quilting gloves
- quilting or tracing paper
- permanent marker

Southwestern Sampler Quilt
designed by Susan Stein and quilted
by Julann Windsperger

Sometimes quilting can be the main focus of the quilt; recently, artists have stitched on a plain or hand-dyed piece of fabric and then used paint, discharge, or paint sticks to color raised areas between stitch lines. At other times, the quilt's piecing or appliqué may be simple and it's the quilting patterns that make it sing. It's important to remember that all quilts benefit from careful quilting to make them durable, beautiful to look at, and cherished by their owners. It's equally important to remember that simple quilting is just as valid as the show-winner's efforts. You should never be afraid to quilt and finish any quilt top that you've made!

Batting varies in density, loft, fiber content, and uses. Cotton and cotton/poly battings are good for bed quilts and garments where some warmth is needed. There are great variations in the density and durability of cotton battings so read labels carefully to learn how far apart to place stitches so the batting launders well. Quilting stitch lines should never be farther apart than 6 inches, but some cotton batting requires more closely placed stitch lines. Very thin polyester battings are sometimes used for garments because they drape better than cotton. Loftier polyester batting is sometimes used for baby quilts where more puff is desired and for tied comforters, but batting fibers may migrate through the fabric. Wool batting is a good choice for warm bed coverings and has been improved for easier laundering. Most importantly, do stitch and wash tests on unfamiliar battings before using them in a project. Some battings benefit from pre-shrinking, but for other projects, post-quilting batting shrinkage can be an attractive effect. Fusible battings take the work out of preparing quilting layers, but cannot be pre-shrunk. Use fusible battings for wall hangings or where you want shrinkage texture and sunken quilting lines.

New threads appear on the market constantly, so buy and try a spool of thread that appeals to you. Different machines, fabrics, and stitching techniques will affect how a thread functions and how easy it is to use. For an important project, always test thread on a scrap of materials before deciding if you want to use that product. For very decorative effects, choose contrasting heavier weight threads like sizes 30 or 40; for more subtle quilting, use matching 50 and 60 weight threads. It's even possible to use heavy threads like perle cotton if you wind it on the bobbin by hand and quilt from the back of your piece. Needle choices will be determined by the kind of thread you use for each project.

When starting out, it may be more comfortable to work with a walking foot on the machine. The foot will act as feed dogs, holding the top of the quilt so the layers feed into the machine evenly. Otherwise, the top layer may be pushed along faster and tucks will form at lines of perpendicular stitching. The walking foot will allow you to do straight and slightly curved lines, but not sharp curves. You can mark a chalk line on your quilt and follow that for a first line of stitching and then use the measuring arms of the walking foot to gauge the distance between subsequent lines.

To start a line of quilting, set the machine for a very short stitch length—do not start at zero or a thread knot will build on the back as you start to stitch. Stitch short stitches for a ½" (1.3 cm) and then set the machine to a normal 10 stitches to the inch. At the end of a line of quilting, dial the stitch length down to almost zero for the last ½" (1.3 cm). If you find that there is excess fabric on the top of the quilt at any point, avoid a tuck by pushing excess

gradually under the walking foot where it will be eased in. Always keep your hands on either side of the presser foot to make sure all the layers feed evenly.

Having the largest, flattest surface around your sewing machine will facilitate easier handling of fabrics. Use an acrylic extension on your sewing machine if you do not have a custom table attachment. Sew on a large table which is smooth and slippery so the quilt moves easily without falling off the table's sides. Polish your machine extension table and surrounding table with furniture wax to remove oil from your hands and remove any fusible build-up that would slow you down. Having a hydraulic chair that can be raised to an optimum height prevents shoulder and back fatigue. Always have plenty of light directed toward your sewing area to help you prevent eye strain and quilt more smoothly. Of course, absence of distractions, good music playing in the background, and pleasant surroundings all help to make quilting more fun, too.

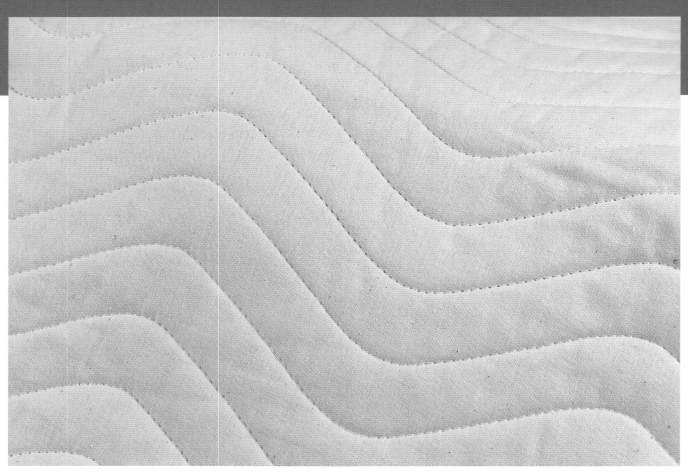

Channel quilting is parallel lines, usually marked beforehand or measured using the walking foot. It works well for making quilted fabric for garment making, since you can stitch the entire length of the fabric from which you will be cutting pattern pieces. For garments, use a batting that drapes well or use fully preshrunk flannel. This example is commercially sold and is useful for quilting placemats, kitchen accessories, and children's clothing.

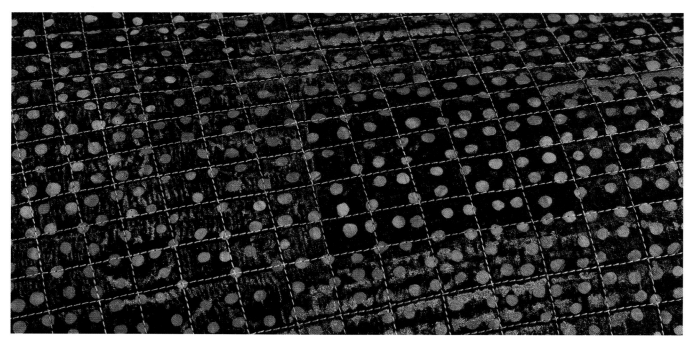

Grid quilting is parallel stitching in both directions. It can be very useful as an allover pattern and can be done in a large grid or in a dense manner as shown here. This sample was painted with a brayer and metallic fabric paint after quilting. Since the stitching is not perfectly straight, the piece has a more relaxed organic appearance.

Stitch-in-the-ditch is quilting done in the seam line of a pieced quilt. Stitch on the low side of the seam where there are no seam allowances underneath. Pressing a quilt top to prepare it for machine quilting requires attention because all seam allowances should be pressed to one side of the seams and should not twist back and forth. They should be pressed without tucks along the stitching, so it's important to press them from the back first and then from the front. Pulling slightly to the sides as the quilt goes under the sewing machine needle helps keep the stitching nestled in the seams.

Free-Motion Quilting

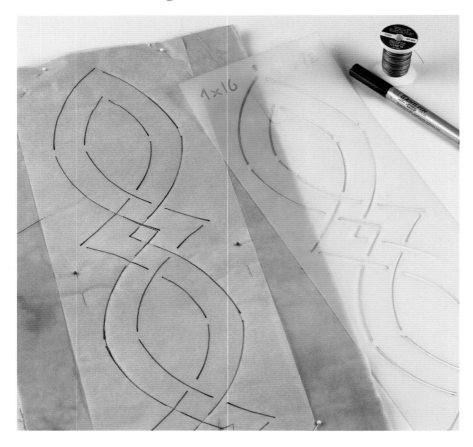

Try the walking foot to create a gentle cable design. Mark the design on tracing/quilting paper (which rips off easily after stitching) with a permanent marker. This technique is especially good for borders because you can do all the fitting of the design into the proper space without making any marks on the quilt itself. Pin paper to the quilt. Quilt over the lines and then remove the paper.

1 Try free-motion quilting if you want the freedom to stitch across an area without following a line or want to add a decorative secondary design to piecing or appliqué. Start with "doodle cloths," so you can relax and work into a comfortable rhythm.

2 Set up the sewing machine by dropping the feed dogs and attaching a "darning foot", which looks like a circle or square with a spring mechanism. As with the walking foot, a darning foot pushes the layers evenly but hops over the surface, compressing the layers only when a stitch is being made. For quilting, a darning spring by itself will not work, since the layers have to be tightly held against the throat plate for a stitch to be made.

3 Remember to lower the presser foot when you start stitching. This step is easy to forget since the foot only holds the layers when the needle is in the fabric. You can usually leave the presser foot down while you are

free-motion quilting and pull the quilt in and out without problems. Use your hands as a hoop, with your hands placed on each side of the needle to keep the layers from shifting. Wearing quilting gloves with sticky finger-tips helps tremendously to reduce strain on your wrists and shoulders.

4 Start and end a line of stitching with ½" (1.3 cm) of very small stitches to tie off the thread. The thread can then be snipped at the surface. When free-motion quilting, rhythm is important, as is running the machine at a fairly fast pace. It will take practice to determine which speed works with which hand movements. Keep your shoulders down and take frequent breaks to avoid muscle fatigue. Make sure surfaces are nice and slippery and that the quilt is supported and not fighting to get away. Roll the quilt to get it under the arm of the machine and make as flat an area as possible around the needle in which to work. Most of all, remember to breathe.

Correct tension

**Bobbin thread shows–
loosen top tension**

**Top thread making loops on back–
tighten top tension**

On a doodle cloth, practice writing your name. When you free-motion quilt, you move the quilt sideways and backwards to make the designs. The orientation of the quilt does not change. Just the same, writing on a piece of paper involves moving the pen, not moving the paper, so a writing-in-stitches exercise will familiarize you with this process. Use two contrasting threads for the exercise so you can readily tell where any adjustments are needed. Be sure to hold the threads when you begin stitching to keep them from knotting on the back.

Echo quilting takes lots of practice but is a good way to tamp down a background and emphasize an appliqué or motif on a fabric. Make concentric circles or a continuous spiral with equal spacing around the motif, shaping the lines to the design. As the lines go farther out from the motif they will become less shaped. Using invisible thread for echo quilting de-emphasizes the thread and accentuates the shadows.

Marking a pattern onto quilting or tracing paper will make practicing free motion easier and harder! Following a line is difficult but doing so gives you a feel for some of the designs commonly used in quilting. Follow the lines with your finger before quilting so you know where the path of the stitching will go. You may want to connect the breaks in the lines inherent with all stencils so you can follow them without hesitation. Machine quilting is like anything else—you have to program your brain in the motions needed to properly accomplish a given task. Also, remember that no one will notice if you went off the lines after the paper is removed!

Another good way to practice free-motion quilting is to quilt around motifs on printed fabric. The outlining does not have to perfectly sit on motif edges but can be interpretive. For a great way to quilt a Trip Around the World quilt or other plain pieced quilt, put a large floral print on the quilt back, and with the quilt reverse side up, quilt around the floral print.

THE COMPLETE PHOTO GUIDE TO TEXTILE ART

Many times you will fill in backgrounds with overall patterns. Draw background design ideas you have seen in books and magazines or at quilt shows. Drawing the designs with a pencil on paper is a good way to practice motions that translate to quilting. Before you start, decide on how dense the quilting will be and then be consistent.

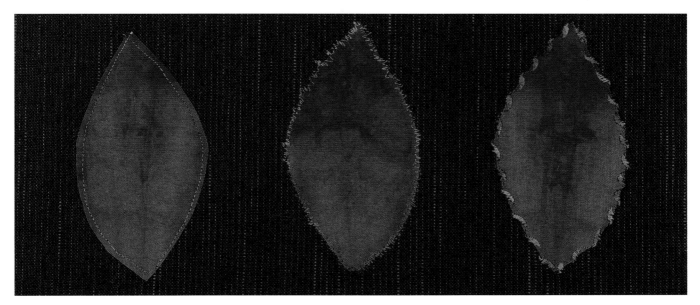

Quilting around the edges of motifs can secure the appliqués and quilt the layers together at the same time. Do all the fusing, gluing, or pinning on the quilt top and then baste, pin, or steam the top, batting, and backing layers together. Straight stitch about ⅛" (3 mm) in from motifs' edges or use a "scribble-stitch" (free-motion zigzag) or programmed stitch to finish the edges. The programmed stitch will require using the feed dogs and a walking foot instead of free-motion techniques.

Gallery for Quilted Effects

Quilt by Sue Kelly. Exciting things have been happening to quilting during the last few years. Artists are making whole cloth quilts with no piecing or appliqué and then painting within the quilted patterns or painting over the entire surface, catching the high points with paint and leaving the quilted indentations the original color. Instead of using a paint brush or brayer to paint quilts, some artists use paint sticks to create subtle effects and not change the fabric's hand. Some quilts are discharged after quilting, leaving stitched lines the original color and removing color on the high points. See the discharging dye chapter for two examples of discharging on finished pieced quilts.

Focus of Quilting

Quilting does not have to be the center of attention on a piece, but it should be done carefully and well so that it enhances the design. Taking a little extra time to custom design a quilting pattern rather than covering the whole piece with meandering (stippling) will raise it from utility quilt to an artistic example of the maker's creativity and the joy a quilter takes in what he or she is doing.

Synergy, a collection of blocks done collaboratively over a year's time by Elizabeth Palmer-Spilker and the author, was skillfully quilted by Sophie Collier. She "scribble-stitched" over all leaf edges, which gives the leaves an organic quality and secures them in the process. Then she did an overall leaf pattern to evenly and beautifully quilt the piece.

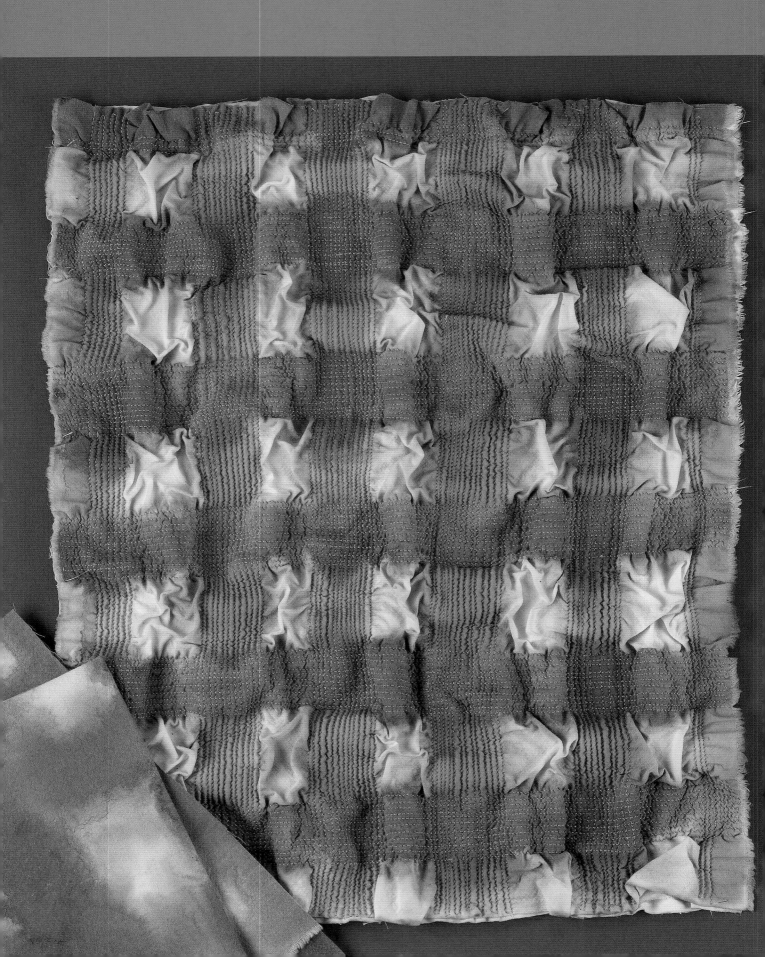

Texturizing Fabric

Texturizing makes fabric attractive, gives it more body, and is a lot of fun to do. The technique requires a top fabric and a shrinking layer, with or without a back, plus lots of stitching.

The shrinking layer can be unwashed muslin or flannel, Solvron Hot-Water Soluble Fabric, Superior's Texture Magic, or wool felt. You can quilt using your free-motion skills or by using the walking foot to do "casual straight lines" in a grid, but you must stitch enough to provide a structure for shrinkage that will create a pattern of hills and valleys. Various stitching densities will make fabric even more dimensional. Since the amount of shrinkage is very unpredictable, make a sample using any materials you are considering for your project.

Texture can be added by pleating instead of shrinking; a striped fabric makes it easy to measure and press pleats before stitching. Choose a bright cotton stripe as shown on page 186, or select a sophisticated woven-stripe garment fabric to create a jacket front.

You don't need to stitch to texturize fabric. It can also be done by tightly twisting the fabric, binding it, and drying it. The crinkles are held in place with fusible interfacing.

Texturizing Basics

Make a sample before you begin your actual project. This piece was affected by the shrinkage of the muslin backing and Solvron in the middle. After being rinsed in hot water, this piece shrunk from 17" x 20" (43 x 51 cm) to 11" x 15" (28 x 38 cm). This textured piece could be used to create a tote front, a pillow, or a matted wall hanging.

1 Layer muslin or other backing fabric, Solvron stabilizer, and a top fabric. Pin across surface.

2 Lay a length of trim or yarn over the top and topstitch it down in a grid or other pattern.

3 Remove the pins and rinse piece in very hot tap water until you see puckering occur. Solvron will dissolve completely in extremely hot water, but will wonderfully pucker in tap water coming from water heaters set at 140°F (60°C). If water is too cool, puckering will not occur.

4 Lay texturized piece on a towel to dry.

If you want less shrinking, for a garment perhaps, use unwashed fabric, such as muslin, for the base and eliminate the Solvron. Preshrink the top layer but do not shrink the muslin. Pin the two layers together and stitch all over the surface, with lines no more than 1½" (4 cm) apart. Machine wash and dry the piece at the highest temperatures. Here you see four test samples: 35% wool/65% rayon felt, flannel, thermal knit, and inexpensive muslin.

Test for Shrinkage

Measure your test samples before shrinking, crinkling, or pleating so you will know the percentage of shrinkage. Figure in this percentage when planning a garment section or other project.

No-Stitch Texture

1. To crinkle fabric without stitching, wet the fabric, blot out excess water, and then gather the fabric into a narrow roll.

2. Holding both ends of the roll, twist in opposite directions until the fabric starts to pull up into a curl.

3 Continue to twist until the roll is formed into a tight ball. Tie the ball or wrap with rubber bands and place in the toe of a sock. Place in the clothes dryer until thoroughly dry.

4 Spread out dry fabric right side down on the ironing board until you see the crinkling you desire.

5 Place fusible interfacing adhesive side down over the crinkled fabric and steam to attach the two layers together.

Pleats

1 To pleat a piece of fabric (this sample was 18" x 42" [45.5 x 106.5 cm] before stitching and about 16" x 14" [38 x 35.5 cm] after) with woven or printed stripes, press on the line between two stripes and then press at intervals that will allow you to easily stitch pleats. On the sample, every third line was pressed.

2 Stitch on the lines at the base of the pleats and then press them to one side. Trim the sides and then stay-stitch sides to hold the pleats in place.

3 Guide the pleats in the opposite direction of how they are pressed and sew across the pleats.

4 Move over a few inches and sew pleats the way they are pressed and then do another stitching with the pleats facing the opposite direction.

5 Add ribbon or trim over the lines of stitching or iron down the pleats for a less dimensional look.

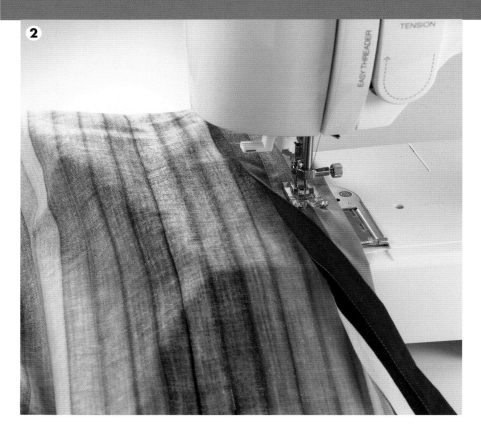

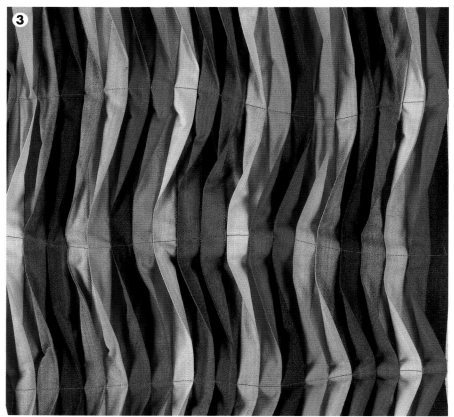

Magic Textures

A new product makes crinkling very easy. Superior Threads has developed a product called Texture Magic, which when sewn to the back of a fabric can be texturized simply by holding a steam iron over it.

1 Pin Texture Magic to the back of the fabric and follow the fabric's design with stitching or do free-motion patterns all over the fabric.

2 Place the piece back side up on the ironing board and hold the iron above the backing. The backing will shrink up and eventually lie flat, leaving the front fabric deeply crinkled.

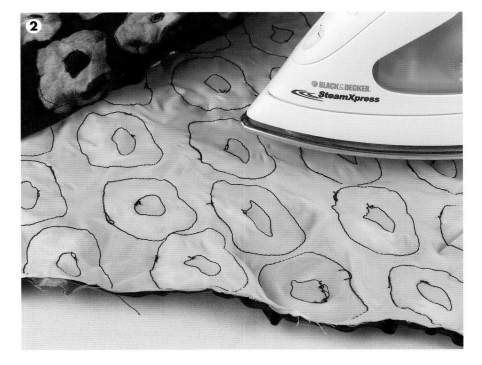

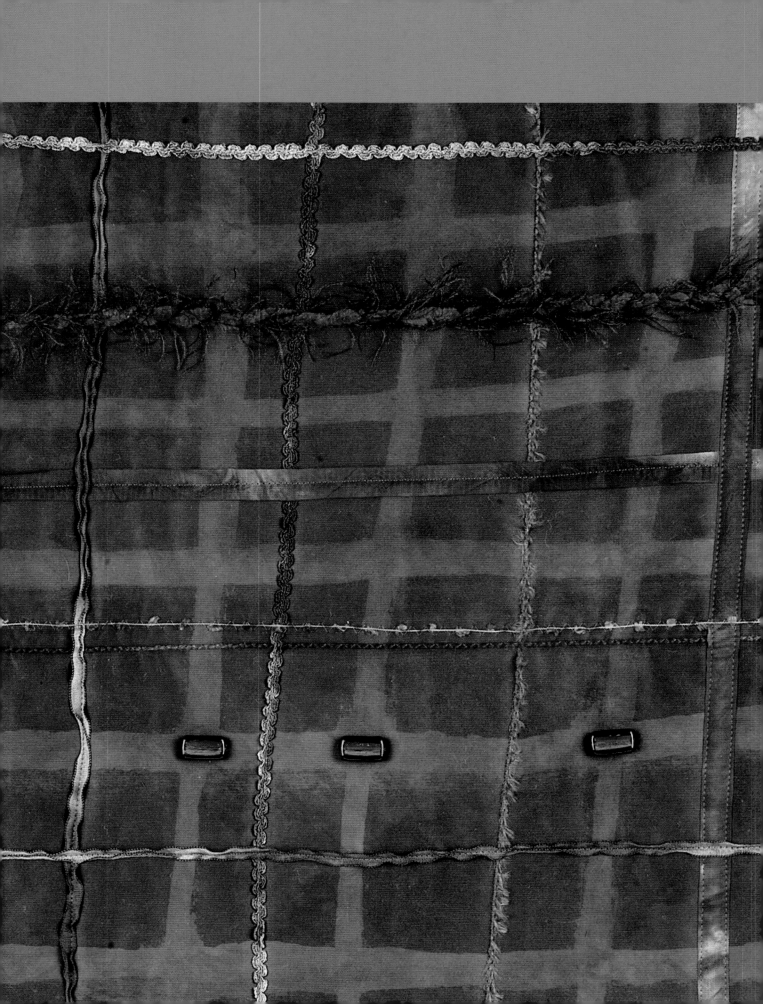

Couching

There are so many gorgeous trims, knitting yarns and tapes, ribbons, and cords on the market that you won't be able to resist adding one or more to a quilt or wall hanging. A plain border benefits from the addition of couched yarn or ribbon and garments are the perfect place for this kind of embellishment.

Since all cords and trims are too heavy to go through the needle of the machine, they must be laid on top of the project and sewn over. Sew them down with decorative effects or simply zigzag over them with invisible thread. There are special feet for sewing on cords and trims but they aren't necessary for success. Use a zigzag foot, walking foot, cording foot, blind hem foot, or zipper foot, depending on the type of trim you are using and which types of presser feet are available. The important thing is to know your favorite color palette and collect complementary ribbons and trims at shows or stores. A broad collection of coordinating embellishments makes a moment of inspiration fruitful, even if that moment occurs at 10 p.m. on Saturday night.

In most cases, you will need to stabilize fabric before couching to prevent puckering. Even a piece of copy paper or newsprint placed behind the fabric can stiffen fabric enough so it easily moves through the machine; once fabric is stitched the stabilizer can be ripped off. Of course, if you are making a quilt with batting, the batting will make a perfect base for couching. As always, test the materials you plan to use before beginning a large project.

YOU WILL NEED

- assorted trims and ribbons
- sewing machine with appropriate presser foot
- matching, decorative, or invisible thread
- large-eyed sewing needles
- fabric stabilizer
- Fray Check (optional)

Couching Basics

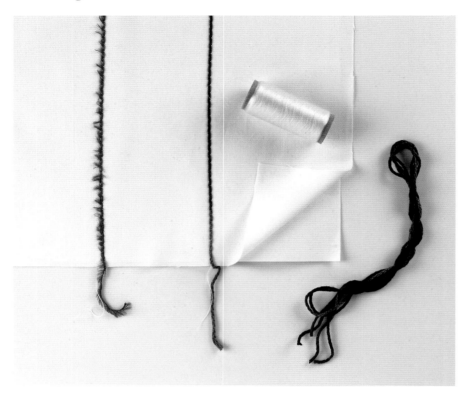

1 Couch over a cord or trim by setting the zigzag stitch wide enough to go into the fabric on either side. The stitch length can be fairly long.

2 Thread the top of the machine with monofilament invisible thread and the bobbin with thread that matches the fabric so it won't show on the top.

3 Leave an inch or two of trim at the edge of the fabric and zigzag over the length of the trim. If you need to start or stop away from an edge, leave a tail of ribbon and thread it onto a large-eye needle and pull it to the back or simply backstitch with the zigzag stitch. Use Fray Check to stop the ribbon or trim from raveling if you leave it on top.

4 When adding ribbons, rickrack, and other wide trims, use a regular straight stitch with monofilament thread and stitch down the center of the trim. With ribbons, this raises up the edges, especially if you have batting in the piece. Stitch down both sides of the ribbon if you want a neater look. If you like, use matching or contrasting sewing thread instead of the invisible thread.

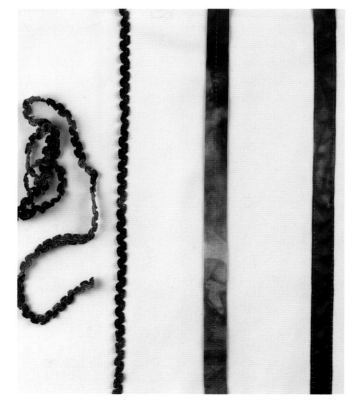

5

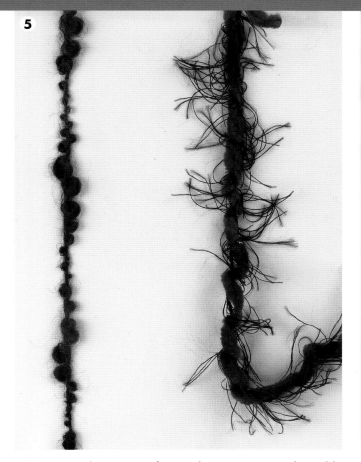

6

5 For yarns that are very fuzzy, where a zigzag stitch would flatten the fibers, use a very-long blind-hem stitch to catch the yarn with the zigzag portion of the stitch sequence. This leaves all the straight stitches lying along the side of the yarn, in the background where they are hidden.

6 For sturdy trims that are difficult to capture by stitching over the top, sew a wide zigzag on the fabric where you will place the yarn. Thread the yarn on a large needle and run it through the stitching.

Using Monofilament

· ·

If you have trouble with monofilament thread feeding off the spool, remove the spool from the machine and put it on a thread stand or in a jar on the floor, where it can unreel freely.

· ·

Bobbin Work

There are wonderful hand-dyed perle cottons, embroidery flosses, and other heavyweight threads too thick to go through the top of the machine and into the needle. These can be hand wound on bobbins, with care being taken to wind them evenly and firmly. The bobbins can then be used in bobbin cases that have been loosened to accommodate the threads' extra thickness.

The top thread can be any thread that matches the fabric's background or invisible thread; the top tension may stay the same as for normal sewing, depending on the effect you want. Experiment with different tensions, and, as always, make a test sample before starting a project.

YOU WILL NEED

- heavy thread
- regular sewing thread
- fabrics
- freezer paper or interfacing
- batting
- walking foot
- darning foot
- sewing machine

Use a walking foot for straight lines, especially if there are layers of fabric and batting, or stabilize your fabric and use a straight stitch foot. As a guide, draw a design on the stabilizer or use a printed fabric with motifs you can follow. For curvy lines and circles, use a darning foot and cover or drop the feed dogs. To start and stop, choose between backstitching, making very small stitches and leaving short tails of thread as decoration, or pulling threads to the back of the work and tying knots. There are many possibilities for using these wonderful heavy threads—possibilities you'll appreciate if you can stand the suspense of sewing from the piece's back and waiting to see the results!

Bobbin-Work Basics

1 Draw a design on a stabilizer like freezer paper or interfacing, or back the fabric with batting and a fabric with a large pattern that can be followed for stitching.

2 Wind thick thread on bobbin by hand. Loosen bobbin case tension so thread moves freely. Insert the bobbin case into the machine.

3 Thread the top of the machine with regular sewing thread. Do a test sample to determine whether you need to change the top or bottom tension. You can go from a neat decorative stitch to a loopy, freeform stitch on the bottom (which will be the top).

4 Place a walking foot on machine and make a line of straight stitching; hang onto both threads when you start stitching.

5 Put on a darning foot and drop or cover the feed dogs on the machine. Working from back of piece, use free-motion stitches to make curves and circles.

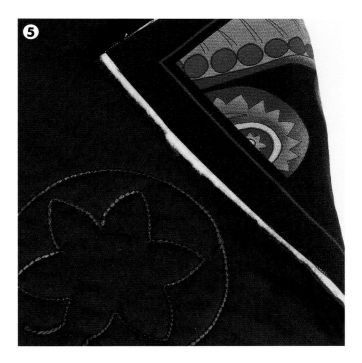

Spare Bobbin Case

Many people designate a second bobbin case for decorative bobbin sewing because they can leave the tension screw loose between projects, and maintain their regular bobbin for normal sewing.

Openwork and Machine Lace

Openwork and machine lace lend themselves to creating fine details on clothing and also to creatively embellishing wall hangings and collages. You can represent a leaf or dragonfly wings with an airy network of veins or create an array of lines within an opening in the fabric to boost interest.

Short Rinse

If you want your lace motif to have body, leave some stabilizer in place by briefly rinsing the piece without completely removing all of the dissolved stabilizer.

Openwork Basics

1 To create an openwork motif, draw a simple frame, in any shape, on fabric.

2 Making sure wrong side of fabric will be against the bed of the machine, place fabric in a hoop at least 1" (2.5 cm) larger all around than the shape. Pull the fabric taut (wrapping the inner hoop with muslin will help hold the fabric) and tighten the screw.

3 Set the machine for a wide satin stitch. Sew around the drawn outline or do three lines of straight stitching on the outline. If you can't get the hoop under the presser foot, remove the foot, slide the hoop underneath, and reattach the foot. (You can also purchase a hoop, with a carved out area, designed for using with a sewing machine.)

4 With a small sharp scissors, carefully cut out the shape inside the stitching.

5 Cut a piece of water soluble stabilizer larger than the drawn shape and pin it around the opening.

6 Set the machine for free-motion stitching and attach a darning foot. Draw with stitches, always starting and stopping stitch lines on the edge of the opening or by attaching them to another line of stitching. Decorate opening edges with more stitching if desired.

7 Cut off the excess stabilizer. Soak the piece in warm water to remove remaining stabilizer. Dry on a towel.

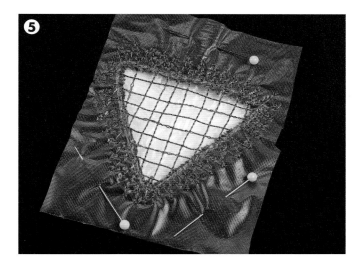

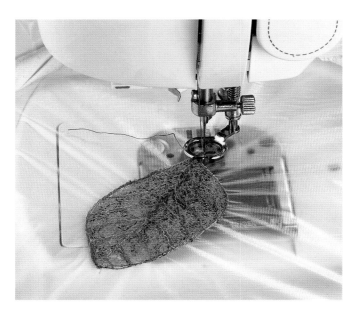

Lace Motifs

1 To make a lace motif that is not attached to fabric, hoop up a piece of water soluble stabilizer.

2 Using lines of straight stitches, outline a leaf, dragonfly wings, or other motif on the stabilizer. Fill in the motif with more stitches. All stitches must be attached to the outline or another line of stitches.

3 Cut off excess stabilizer and rinse piece in warm water.

4 Reshape the motif and lay on a towel to dry.

5 Attach motif to a collage or other project using a few tacking stitches placed so the motif edges remain free.

Thread Painting

Thread painting or free-motion embroidery is a great way to create an image that has lots of texture and detail. It is much like drawing or tracing an outline and then shading it in with a pencil—but you will have a permanent and colorful result on fabric!

Any sewing machine that makes a straight stitch and drops the feed dogs (or covers them) will work for this technique. Similar to the technique used for creating machine lace, thread painting is done on fabric rather than just on stabilizer. Fabric can be printed, hand-dyed, photo transferred, stamped, or stenciled or the thread painting can be added to plain fabric.

The abundance of different threads allows for a myriad of interpretations of an image. Rayon, metallic, polyester, silk, and cotton threads all have their own characteristics and can be mixed for different effects and light reflection. Heavy threads—numbers 12 and 30—stand out and are good for outlining. Fine threads—numbers 60 and 50—are good for fill-in shading and subtle details. Needles should be matched to threads. Use large needles (14 and 16) for metallic and heavy threads and smaller needles (12 and 14) for finer threads. Usually a number 60-weight bobbin thread can be used in the bobbin to allow fewer stops, but if the back will be seen, the bobbin thread can match the top thread. Top thread tension will need to be adjusted for best stitch appearance and to prevent breakage. Always do a test sample before beginning a project.

YOU WILL NEED

- stabilizers
- fabrics
- embroidery hoop
- sewing machine
- darning foot
- quilting gloves
- thread

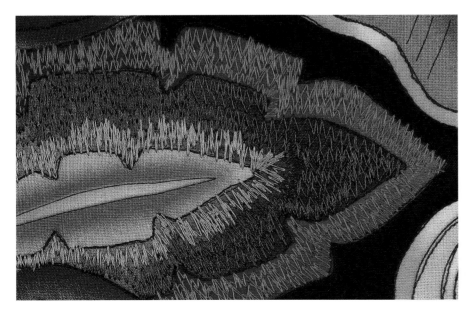

Use a photo transfer or printed commercial fabric for your base.

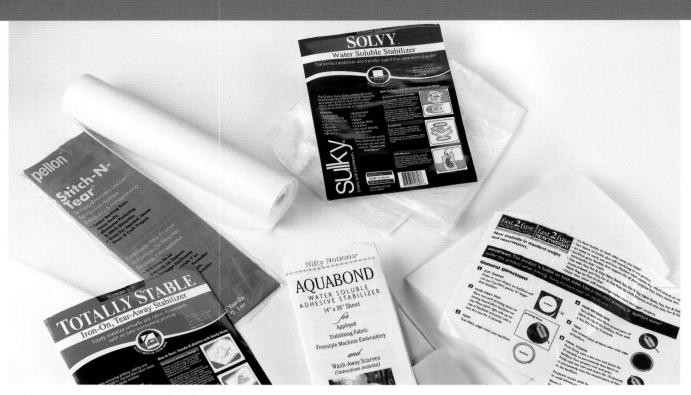

Stabilizing is necessary for thread painting/machine embroidery; stabilizing ensures that fabric does not pucker with the extensive stitching required for this technique. The method for stabilizing fabric varies according to the project's end use. If you will be framing the piece, you can use a stiff interfacing, either fusible or applied with temporary adhesive, and will not need to use a hoop. If you are making a garment or quilted project, you will want to use a temporary stabilizer so it can be removed after stitching is complete and leave the fabric flexible. Tear-away stabilizers can be purchased in different weights, but you could also use newsprint or other paper that rips easily. Water-soluble stabilizers come in sheets that look like plastic. Heat-away stabilizers are ironed off after stitching is complete. You will probably need a hoop in conjunction with the tear-away, water-soluble, or heat-away stabilizers. Make sure your fabric is compatible with the stabilizer's removal method. If you wish, layer the top, batting, and backing and embroider through all layers without a hoop. This works well for a pillow top or other projects where the back will not show.

Thread-Painting Basics

To choose a hoop for a project, pick one small enough to maneuver under the arm of the machine, but large enough so you don't have to move it often. There are special hoops with carved out areas that allow the hoops to slip under the presser foot, but a regular wooden hoop will also work if you remove the presser foot each time you move the hoop from under the needle.

1 Wrap the inner hoop with strips of muslin to tightly grasp the fabric.

2 Lay the fabric right side up over the outer hoop and then push the inner hoop down inside; keep the fabric straight and taut. Tighten the screw on the hoop.

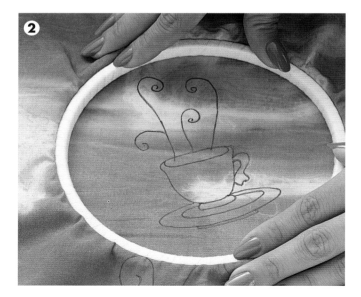

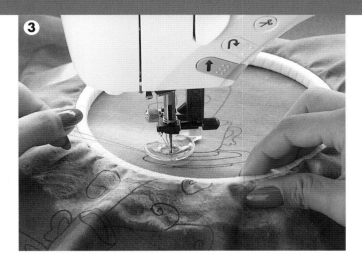

3 Set up the machine by winding the bobbin with 60-weight thread (if it won't show) and threading the top with decorative thread. Check the tension to make sure the bobbin thread does not come up to the top surface. If it does, turn the top tension to a lower number.

4 Place a darning foot on the machine and drop the feed dogs. If you can't drop the feed dogs, punch a hole in a business card and tape it over the feed dogs so the needle will go through the hole.

5 Lower the presser foot bar and leave it down because this step is easy to forget when you have a darning foot on the machine.

6 For a project that is not in a hoop, use quilting gloves with non-slip fingertips to maneuver the fabric. Place your hands on both sides of the needle and use a fast, steady motor speed along with a smooth movement of the fabric to get consistent stitch length. Pay attention to your shoulders and wrists and take frequent breaks. Raising or lowering your chair and tilting the machine towards you with rubber erasers under the back can alleviate muscle fatigue. Also remember to breathe!

7 For a project in a hoop, hold the hoop lightly and move it under the needle with smooth motions while running the motor at a consistent speed. It is much easier to make regular stitches when you are going faster rather than too slowly.

8 Start and stop stitching lines with tiny stitches. Outline an area with straight stitches and then fill in with side to side stitches; using a wide zigzag setting may help when filling in large areas. Feather edges of different colored areas so they blend smoothly.

9 Remove stabilizer following manufacturer's directions.

Thread Samplers

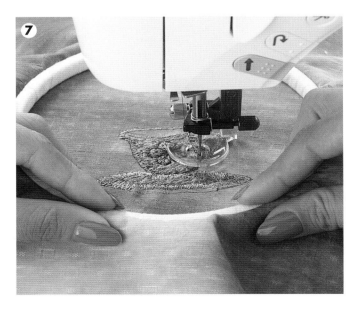

Buying thread samplers at quilt shows allows you to get small spools of thread in many colors, which can be used to create appealing shading using threads with different values of the same color.

Appliqué

Any motif added to the top of a fabric can be considered an appliqué. There are numerous methods, from gluing to hand-sewing, for applying motifs to fabric. There is at least one application method that appeals to every style of fabric artist. The only "rule" in appliqué is that the workmanship must make the added motif durable enough for the project's intended purpose. Something meant to be displayed on a wall can be constructed differently than a piece intended for a child's quilt or garment.

On this sample, the silks were painted, heat set, and backed with woven fusible interfacing, and then the Double Wedding Ring pattern was pieced. The appliquéd flowers were not backed but were roughly cut and then singed in a candle flame to seal the edges and add an attractive gray edge. The flowers were topstitched to the pieced top after it was layered with the batting and backing, which added stability and dimension.

TURNED-EDGE APPLIQUÉ

Turned-edge appliqué is the traditional appliqué method, but it can be executed in different ways to utilize a sewing machine. When using a sewing machine for turned-edge appliqué, secure the appliqué edges before you go to the sewing machine.

YOU WILL NEED

- water-resistant cardboard
- scissors
- fabric
- starch
- sewing machine
- zigzag foot
- invisible or matching thread

This sample was pieced in the usual way, but to add dimension, strips were added over the top in a diagonal grid pattern. The strips can be easily made by sewing a 2 ½"-wide (6.5 cm) strip of fabric, with right sides facing out, into a tube. Cut a ⅞" (2.2 cm) piece of heavy cardboard wide and run it through the fabric tube while steam pressing to place the seam allowances on the back of the tube and to create straight edges. Slide the cardboard inside the tubes as you press until you have enough fabric lengths for your project.

Turned-Edge Appliqué Basics

Cut out a template for an appliqué motif, in its finished size, from heavy cardboard. Food packages with a slightly shiny coating, like pasta boxes, work well because they won't fall apart when wet.

1 Lay appliqué fabric, wrong side up, on an ironing board. Place the cardboard template on top. Cut out the fabric shape, adding a scant ¼" (6mm) seam allowance all around. Clip inside corners and curves to the edge of the cardboard.

2 Dab liquid starch, either from a spray can or diluted from a bottle, on the seam allowance. Use the tip of a dry iron to press seam allowance up and over the back of the template. When the seam allowance is dry, move on to the next area of fabric. To make the edges curve smoothly, do small areas at a time.

3 Pop the cardboard template out of the fabric. Securely pin the appliqué to background fabric and set up the machine for blind-hemming. The bobbin thread should match the background fabric and the top thread should match the appliqué or be invisible monofilament. A short stitch length and medium stitch width should work for most projects. The goal is to have the zigzag portion of the stitch fall ⅛" (3 mm) to ³/₁₆" (.48 cm) apart and have the width wide enough so you can catch the edge of the appliqué easily.

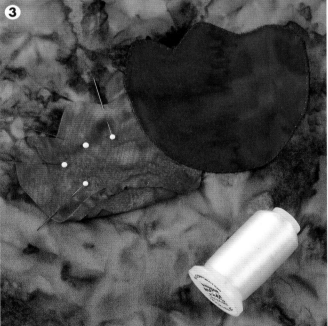

4 Place a piece of newsprint or tracing paper behind the background fabric to prevent puckering. Sew around the appliqué, with the straight stitches of the sequence falling on the background and the zigzag stitches catching the edge of the appliqué. The paper will tear off easily after stitching is complete.

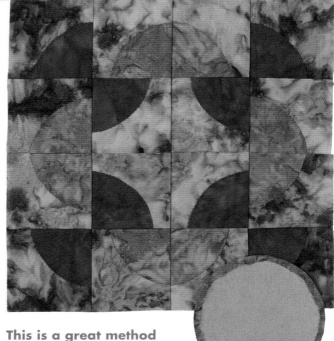

This is a great method for making Drunkard's Path blocks. Prepare 5" (12.5 cm) circles with starch and appliqué them to 7" (18 cm) background squares. Cut the squares into fourths and reassemble into quilt blocks.

This piece, made by Elizabeth Palmer-Spilker, employs blind-hem stitching on the graduated colors of the background, with faced appliqués tucked into the seams and left free around the edges. Beads add wonderful texture to this small wall hanging.

Trimming

For any kind of appliqué, cutting away the background fabric underneath the appliqués is optional. It primarily depends on whether you want to reduce the bulk or whether the appliqué fabric is lighter in value than the background, which can create a shadow.

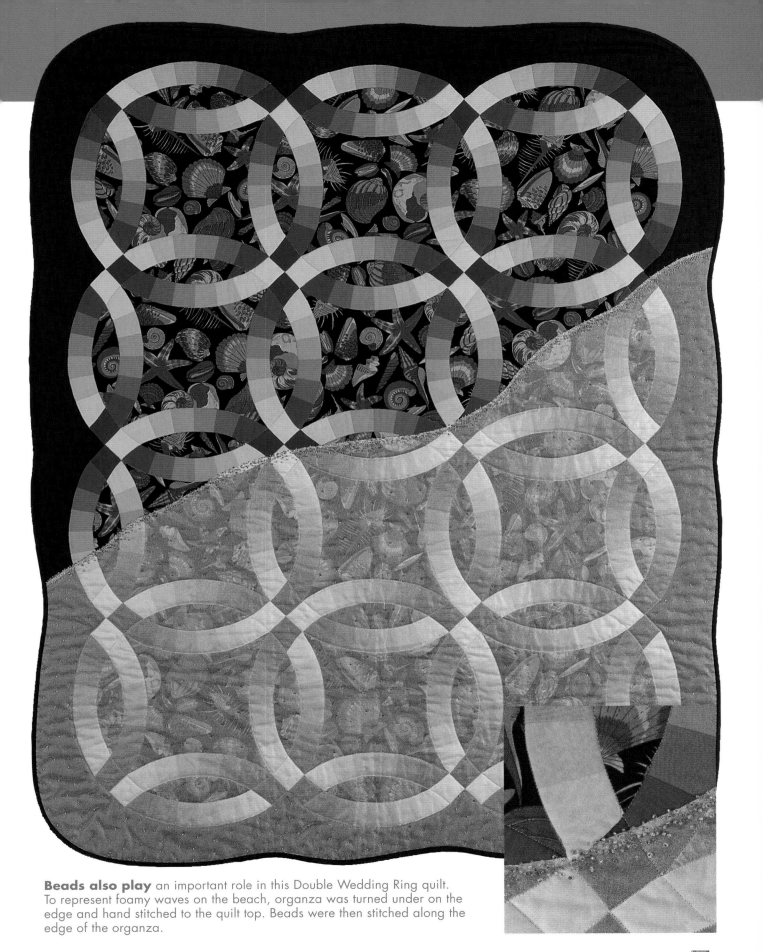

Beads also play an important role in this Double Wedding Ring quilt. To represent foamy waves on the beach, organza was turned under on the edge and hand stitched to the quilt top. Beads were then stitched along the edge of the organza.

RAW-EDGE AND FUSED APPLIQUÉ

Raw edges on appliqué add texture and interest and can be just as durable for daily use as turned-edge appliqué. For wall pieces, raw edges give the viewer something that will be hard for them to resist touching! Edges can be intentionally frayed or just allowed to ravel slightly. Or, the motifs can be fused with web adhesives to the background and no fraying will occur. Fusing can stiffen fabric but does prevent slippage while stitching. Determine the edge style you want before you choose the final technique.

YOU WILL NEED

- fabrics
- batting (optional)
- sewing machine
- darning foot
- glue stick or white glue in needle-nose bottle
- pins
- Wonder-Under fusible web
- Misty Fuse adhesive web
- trims, ribbons, buttons, or beads
- thread

This wall piece resulted from a class I took with Vicki Johnson many years ago in California. The mountains, rocks, and foreground were painted before any appliqué was added. The cacti were pinned in place and topstitched close to the edges. To make three-dimensional spines, tacking stitches were scattered around the cacti and then the thread connecting them was cut. Thread painting adds detail to the flowers and makes grass and flowers for the background. All the quilting, topstitching, and thread painting were done through the batting and backing to add depth.

Raw-Edged Appliqué Basics

Overdyed fabrics by Diane Swallen and Wendy Richardson

1 Cut out shapes from any fabric or printed motifs from large florals. Remember that some printed fabrics have very white backs so if the edges curl, the white will show.

2 Pin motifs to a background fabric or use glue stick on the back edges to hold the fabric pieces in place. A very thin bead of white glue can also be used; just be careful to use only enough to hold or it will impede the stitching. Let the glue dry.

3 Set the sewing machine for free-motion stitching (feed dogs down or covered, darning foot on) and topstitch around the motifs ⅛" (3 mm) in from the edges. If you are using denim, corduroy, or other heavy fabrics, two or three lines of stitching are recommended. Stitches should be firm with even tension. Use matching or contrasting thread. If you wish, layer batting and backing under the background so the quilting will be accomplished at the same time as the appliqué. If a lot of texture is desired, brush raw edges with a suede brush or machine wash and dry, pulling threads off midway through the wash cycle.

A quilt with raw edges left exposed sometimes reinforces the theme of the piece; in this case, transitions and emotions.

This wall quilt or table runner goes even further with free edges. The leaves were cut from hand-dyed fabric so backs and fronts would be the same color (batik fabric would also work) and then glue-sticked temporarily to the background. The "casually straight" quilting lines spaced every ½" (1.3 cm) are the only stitches holding the leaves. After 15 years, the leaves are still intact and have developed a natural-looking curl.

Collages are fun to make with a collection of materials that harmonize in color or theme. Add large elements to the background fabric, embellish with ribbons or cut strips and squares, and then add smaller embellishments like buttons or beads. The evolving quality of collage lends itself well to the flexibility of raw edge appliqué. By stitching everything on after the batting and backing layers are added, further quilting becomes optional.

Fused Appliqué Basics

Fusible appliqué is hugely popular because it eases construction. Paper-backed webs, like Wonder-Under by Pellon, are good foundations for drawing patterns, and Misty Fuse is wonderful for fusing sheer fabrics, and since it isn't sticky, for projects where the entire surface is not covered.

1 Iron the web onto the back of appliqué fabrics following manufacturer's directions.

2 Cut out motifs freehand or trace patterns onto the release paper of the paper-backed products. For Misty Fuse, draw a design with a #2 pencil onto parchment paper, cover with web, and place a fabric, right side up, over the top. Iron the layers and the markings will transfer from the parchment to the webbed fabric.

3 Iron the backed appliqué to the background fabric, using steam. For some paper-backed webs, caution is necessary to avoid "cooking" the web, which makes it come up through the fabric and turn stiff. Test any products before using them in a project. Fused appliqués require no further work if the piece will be hung on a wall, but should be edge-stitched if laundering is a possibility. Sewing 1/8" (3mm) from the edge is sufficient unless a more decorative effect is desired.

Satin stitch around the edges of an appliqué by setting the machine for a medium stitch width and very short stitch length—stitching should cover the edge for the most attractive effect. Attach an appliqué foot and stitch along the edge of the motif, avoiding wandering onto the background. You can also use a decorative stitch like a feather or buttonhole stitch—these stitches won't cover the edge completely, which doesn't present a problem when working with fused appliqué.

The fused appliqué can also be finished with couching. Set a cord or yarn along the edges and apply with the methods illustrated in the Couching chapter. This sample features inkjet-printed silk organza fused to felt with Misty Fuse that was colored with Pearl Ex powder and foiled. Rubber-stamp-embossed Angelina film was then fused with Misty Fuse to the organza. Eyelash trim was couched around the edges with ends left to dangle.

Stabilize

Any time you are stitching heavily around the edges of an appliqué, stabilize the background fabric by placing a piece of newsprint or tracing paper behind it. The bobbin thread will be less apparent and the fabric won't pucker.

LINED APPLIQUÉ

Lined appliqué allows you to create more dimensional appliqués. The motif edges are fully enclosed and the backs can be used as part of the design. You can even put wire into the appliqués for easy shaping.

The front and back fabrics can be the same, or for more interest, use two different fabrics. Since the top fabric will be supported you can use a sheer or specialty fabric or include batting in the construction to add substance.

Lined Appliqué Basics

1 Draw the finished outline of the appliqué motifs on the back side of one fabric; leave at least ½" (1.3 cm) between motifs.

2 Place the two fabrics right sides together and pin. Sew on the drawn lines with a short stitch length, stitching over the beginning stitches to secure.

3 Cut out the motifs with a scant ¼" (6mm) seam allowance outside the stitched line. Trim off outside corners and cut up to the seam lines of inside corners. Cut a slit in the center of the back fabric, being careful not to cut into the top fabric.

4 Turn the motif right side out through the slit and slide a bone folder or knitting needle around the inside to push out the the appliqué's edges and points. Press the motifs.

5 Sew the appliqués to the background so they stand out on the edges. If you like, encourage curling of the edges with an iron or your fingers.

Another Option

Lined appliqué can also be used as another way to turn under the edges before attachment to the background fabric. In this case, a lightweight fabric, such as netting, interfacing, or organza, is usually used for the back. The finished motif is sewn to the background in the same way as turned-under appliqués—by using a blind-hem machine stitch or hand stitching. See page 203 for instructions on flat appliqué.

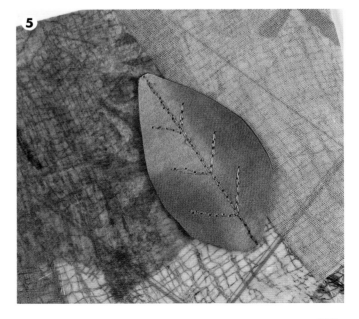

REVERSE APPLIQUÉ AND CUTWORK

Sometimes it is advantageous to appliqué by cutting through the top layer of fabric to reveal one or more underlying layers. Tiny shapes are easier to reveal using reverse, hand appliqué methods than turned-edge appliqué because you don't have to wrestle with uncooperative seam allowances.

This technique is used to create intricately patterned molas of San Blas Islands in Panama, which are collected around the world for their unique look. Dramatic stained glass effects can be accomplished with a filigree of black fabric overlaying a colorful background. And a scenic fabric or photo transfer can look dimensional when seen through a cutout window. There are cutwork patterns that look like wrought iron fences in front of a garden scene and others that look like church windows.

YOU WILL NEED

• fabrics for top layer and feature layer

• Wonder-Under fusible web

• craft knife or small scissors

• freezer paper

• thread for appliqué

This cutwork piece is by Elizabeth Palmer-Spilker of Columbus, Ohio. She fused the black cutout over a shibori fabric by Lunn Fabrics and then quilted to echo the style of the black fabric design.

This particular mola has a lot of laid-on, turned-edge appliqué, but the long green outline is reverse appliquéd, which means the black fabric is turned under a thread or two and the edge is stitched so finely it is difficult to see the thread or stitches. This is a piece sold to tourists. Large molas were originally used as fronts for blouses. Mola patterns usually represent flowers, birds, and other fauna of Panama.

Reverse Appliqué Basics

1 Cut a tightly woven black fabric to the size of your feature fabric and back with fusible web, such as Wonder-Under, using a dry iron.

2 Draw a design onto the release paper, remembering that the design will be reversed when you place it over the feature fabric. With a craft knife or scissors, cut out the areas that will be removed and save them to fuse to another project.

3 Peel the release paper from the web and position the black design over the feature fabric. Steam-iron the black cutout to the feature fabric. You can edge-stitch the black fabric if you wish or stitch over it as you quilt.

Cut a window silhouette out of black and fuse it over a scenic fabric or photo transfer. On the sample, where a critter's head was hidden by the window frame, the black fabric was trimmed closely around it before fusing.

Freezer-Paper Overlay

Another way to do an overlay is to draw a design onto the non-shiny side of freezer paper, and then cut out the negative spaces.

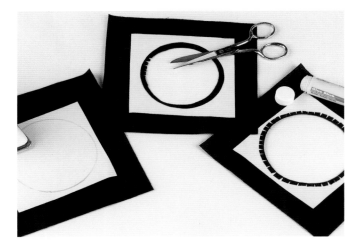

1 Iron the freezer paper with drawn design to the back of the uppermost fabric.

2 Cut out negative spaces from the fabric with a craft knife or small scissors, leaving scant seam allowances around the edges of the openings. Clip into the inside corners and curves, cutting up to the edges of the freezer paper. Glue-stick the seam allowances to the non-shiny side.

3 Place the cut-out piece over the feature fabric and sew along the turned-under edges by hand or machine.

4 Cut away the feature fabric hidden by the uppermost fabric and pull out the freezer paper.

This wonderful little piece by Elizabeth Spilker is made from just two pieces of fabric—the top brown layer that makes the tree and border and the striped piece used for the background. Elizabeth used an open zigzag stitch to finish the interior edges and a wider closed zigzag to finish the outside edges of the piece

Easy Art

Sew a number of brightly colored fabric strips together and press. Make a piece of black filigree and fuse it over the strips—it will be just like creating the crayon-scratching pictures from your childhood!

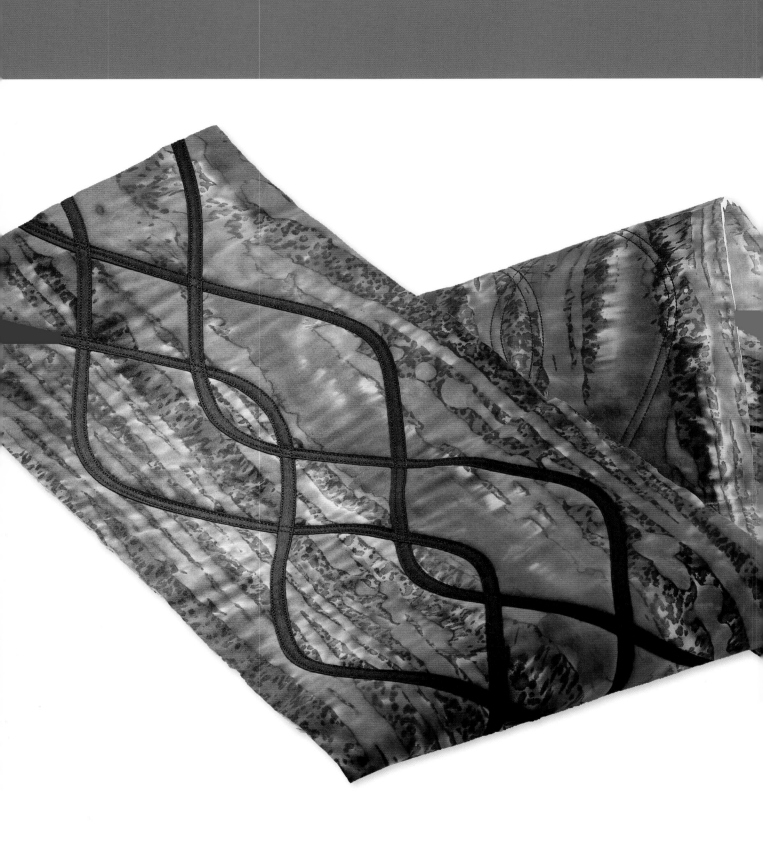

Bias Strip Appliqué

Bias strip appliqué is very useful for creating dynamic designs, as in stained glass appliqué, Celtic knot designs, crazy quilted looks, and stems for floral patterns.

Bias strips can be purchased with fusible web applied to the back or as double-fold bias tape, which can be trimmed down to the required ¼" (6 mm) plus seam allowances. You can also make your own bias strips by sewing a tube of fabric and pressing it flat with a heat-proof bar.

YOU WILL NEED

- cotton fabrics
- muslin
- fusible web
- fusible bias tape or double-fold bias tape, ¼" (6mm) wide
- sewing machine
- thread
- bias pressing bar, ¼" (6mm) (or stiff cardboard strip)

A quilting stencil was used to mark a cable design on this border and then bias tape was fused in place and sewn down to quilt the three layers at the same time.

Bias Strip Appliqué Basics

1 Cut a crazy quilt block or simple landscape out of fabrics backed with fusible web. Place pieces on a foundation square of muslin, aligning piece edges, and fuse.

2 Cover the pieces' edges with fusible bias tape and iron down. Or, use double-fold bias tape with the wider fold trimmed off and pin it in place. Be sure all ends are covered with a subsequent line of bias tape or fall at the edge of the block.

3 Sew down both edges of the bias tape with matching thread, stopping and starting stitching lines in the interior of the block with tiny stitches to lock the thread.

1

2

3

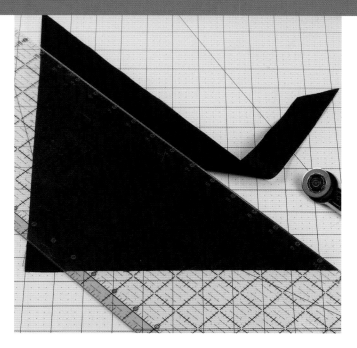

To make your own ¼" (6 mm) bias tape, cut bias strips 1" (2.5 cm) wide, fold them in half lengthwise with wrong sides together, and sew with a scant ¼" (6 mm) seam allowance. Cut seam allowances down to ⅛" (3 mm) and insert a ¼" (6 mm) bias press bar into the tube (do not turn the tube). Press the tube flat while sliding the bar along inside, while keeping the seam on the back where it will be hidden.

Shiny Choices

Fusible bias tape also comes in silver and gold metallic finishes and is perfect for making beautiful holiday decorations.

Needle Felting

Needle felting bonds two fabrics or fibers together through the use of barbed needles, which tangle the fibers to make a fascinating new textile. Wet felting is a different process during which water and soap are used to cause wool fibers to migrate and tangle with each other to create fabric. A third type of felting is the shrinking of knitted items or loosely woven wool by washing in hot water.

Needle felting can be done entirely by hand using one or more barbed needles and a thick foam pad to punch into. Multiple needle holders speed up the process of punching fibers together, while a single needle allows precise placement of fiber and great detail. Many people use an embellisher machine, which is like a sewing machine with no bobbin, no thread, and multiple barbed needles. Some regular sewing machines can be adapted for needle felting by adding a special array of attachments and removing the bobbin assembly. Check with your sewing machine dealer for more information.

Felting of any kind is usually done with wool roving, fabric, and yarn because wool has naturally barbed fibers that successfully bond with each other. Other fibers and fabrics can also be combined with wool or used alone to produce fascinating felted effects; felting is being used to create all kinds of new textures and techniques. Look at yarn stores for gorgeous materials newly available to knitters.

If you choose to do felting by hand, insert up to six needles into the needle holder handle and screw the top down firmly. Place a thick foam pad on the table and set a piece of fabric to be embellished or wool fibers on the foam. Punch the needles into the wool over and over, taking care to avoid injury from the barbed needles. The fibers will quickly tangle together or attach to the background. Nothing else is required to make the new fabric durable for use as clothing, pillows, or other decorative or wearable items. Fabrics that you can felt into include anything firmly woven like wool, synthetic and wool felt, velveteen, denim, silk, and cotton. Avoid hard materials that might break the needles. Wool fibers can be felted together without any fabric involved, but using a piece of netting inside the layers may build a stronger piece of felt.

YOU WILL NEED

- wool roving
- yarns and trims, with fuzzy texture
- fabrics like wool, velveteen, synthetic and wool felt, and denim
- organza and other sheer fabrics
- fine nylon net
- print fabric
- size 36 felting needles
- handle for holding multiple needles
- embellisher machine (optional)
- heat gun

Purse knitted and shrunk by Rosi Igo, fibers by Pagewood Farm, hand needle felted by author.

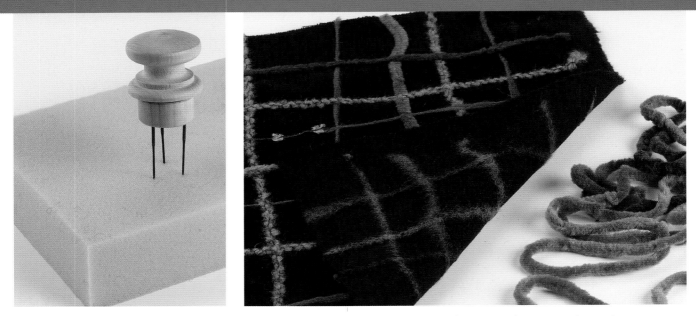

Make a sampler of different yarns and trims by laying them on a piece of cotton velveteen and punching over them with hand needles or an embellisher. No thread is used. Needles push the trims' fibers through the fabric, causing them to stay embedded. Some trims will prove too fragile for this process, like the eyelash trim pictured here. Check the back of the fabric—sometimes the softer effect on the back is very attractive and just as useful as the front.

Punch wool trim or yarn into a piece of felt. Turn the felt over after all the trim is attached and punch over some lines from the back. Here, the shorter lines were felted from the back, causing the black felt to come to the top and alter the appearance of the trim.

Stack a piece of wool and a piece of cotton fabric. With cotton side up, punch through the fabrics. Here, cotton organza's broken fibers come through the wool fabric. The heavier quilter's cotton in the other sample stays intact for a more subtle effect on the wool layer. Try different combinations of front and back needling for a variety of effects.

Needle Felting Basics

Attach wool roving to synthetic felt.

1 Hold your hands apart and pull the wool roving into pieces rather than cutting it. Separate roving into manageable tufts and lay it onto the felt.

2 Cover with thin netting to hold wool in place while you stitch. Punch over the piece with a felting needle or embellisher to embed the fiber in the felt. Punching from the front will embed the roving in the felt and punching from the back will attach the netting.

3 After felting is finished, melt the netting with a heat gun, being careful not to melt the felt underneath the roving.

1

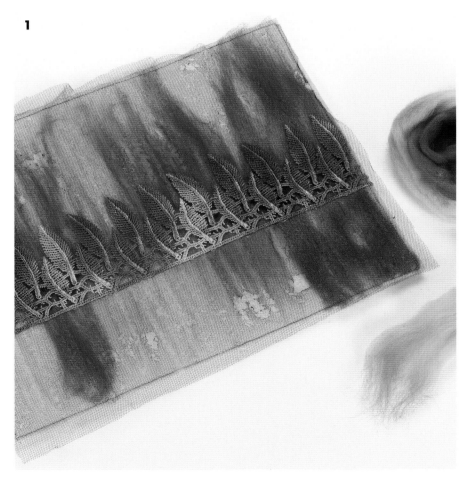

Felt on felt. Lay pieces of cut felt onto a background of felt. Needle until the pieces are bonded to the background. Remember to punch from both the back and the front for a variety of looks.

Vary the view. Place a print fabric on top of a piece of wool or felt, cover with netting, and punch from the back to bond the fabrics together and create a pattern on front.

Lay out wool roving between draped layers of netting, leaving some of the netting empty, and needle felt by hand or machine. The barbed needles may tear holes in the netting while felting the wool. Melt some of the netting with a heat gun. Couch eyelash trim over the top of the netting. Sew the piece to a collaged background so parts of the background peek through the netting.

Lay yarn in a pattern on a background and punch it in. Fill in the outline with roving and punch it in.

Cut shapes from fabric, such as velvet, and punch into a wool background. Lay yarn around the shapes and punch them in to accentuate the shapes.

Punch wool roving into felt from the front until it is firmly attached. Turn the felt over and punch from the back to bring lines of the background color to the front, checking often to see the effect you're creating. Try to maintain a fluid feeling. You can steam the piece after felting to smooth it and slightly close the punch holes. Always leave extra fabric around your motif so you can straighten edges—punching will usually distort the background.

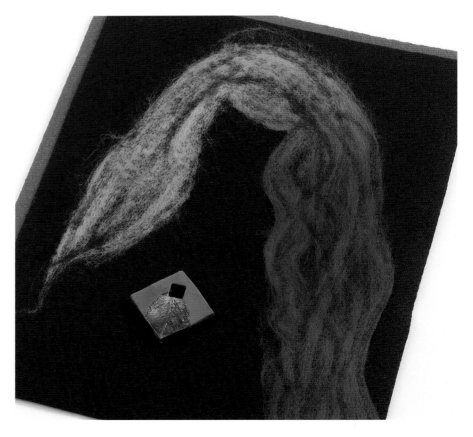

Tear strips of synthetic and silk sheer fabrics, set them on a synthetic felt background, and punch down the centers of the strips. The needles gather the strips as you punch and create more dimension. Use a heat gun to melt the synthetic strips and the felt. Be sure to work in a well-ventilated area or outside.

Tip

Try to keep the embellisher moving quickly; going slowly while moving the materials may result in needle breakage. When hand felting, punch straight down and attach any beads or other hard embellishments after you are done punching.

Sheer Layers

There are many gorgeous natural-fiber and synthetic sheer fabrics on the market. Buy small amounts of different sheer fabrics to play with. Add texture to the fabrics; layer the sheers over each other; cut through the layers to reveal colors underneath; or burn through some layers to expose others. These techniques avoid the use of acrylic medium or fusible web which stiffen the materials.

YOU WILL NEED

- silk sheers, such as organza and net organza
- synthetic sheers, such as nylon, chiffon scarves, tulle, polyester, and netting
- cotton or other foundation layers
- painted or dyed cheesecloth
- Misty Fuse adhesive web
- heat gun
- beads, buttons, or other embellishments
- beading thread and needle
- sewing machine
- thread
- stuffing or wool roving
- tracing paper (optional)
- natural materials, Angelina shreds, skeleton leaves, or other dimensional items

Sheer Layers Basics

1 Cut a cotton foundation fabric.

2 Drape cheesecloth over the foundation. Insert Misty Fuse pieces underneath cheesecloth, place cooking parchment on top, and fuse.

3 Foil the Misty Fuse that isn't covered by cheesecloth.

4 Cut a piece of nylon sheer larger than the foundation. With a heat gun, shrink circles into the nylon.

5 Place circle-patterned nylon over the cheesecloth and sew down the sides to hold in place.

6 Hand bead shrunken areas on nylon. As always, add a button or bead as "fiber art jewelry" to give the composition a focal point.

Dimensional Circles

1 On a piece of iridescent sheer fabric, sew circles using a long stitch length and sturdy thread, leaving long thread tails. To make it easier to sew, draw circles onto tracing paper and place paper under the sheer. After all the circles are sewn, tear off the paper.

2 Pull up the thread to gather the circles and tie off the thread on the back.

3 Stuff the bubble-like circles with polyester stuffing or colored wool roving.

4 Stitch circle-patterned sheer fabric to a complementary foundation fabric.

Finding Fabrics

Old chiffon scarves are the sheerest fabric. Look for them at garage sales and ask relatives if they have some tucked away. Nylon netting is the next best thing for showing the layers underneath. Metallic-looking materials will reflect light and hide what is covered.

Some materials may seem unsuitable for a fabric project, but when topped with sheer layers they can be beautiful and unique. Angelina, Mylar, handmade paper, buttons and beads, natural materials, and loose silk fibers are just some of the items that can be "trapped" under a sheer fabric. Place the materials on a firmly woven foundation, with or without batting and backing, cover with sheer fabric, pin, and sew around them and through all the layers to secure. Shibori square by Glennis Dolce

On a piece of batting, lay natural and synthetic sheers. Here, a curtain fabric, velvet devore, cheesecloth, and metallic organza were layered. Cover the sheers with nylon netting and pin in place. Sew across the surface of the layers with cotton thread. Melt some netting with a heat gun or cut through it with a scissors. The decorated ribbon was added afterward. Ribbon by Wendy Richardson.

For Cyndi Kaye Meier's Labyrinth #5, multiple layers of silk were hand-dyed with Procion MX dyes. Then the fabric was screen printed and painted with Jacquard Textile Color. Painted upholstery cord was applied and machine and hand stitching were added after layering with interfacing instead of batting in order to maintain the sheer quality while stabilizing the piece.

Resources

Angelina shreds and film:
www.embellishmentvillage.com

Beijie paper, Chinese calligraphy paper,
watercolor crayons, and other art supplies:
www.jerrysartarama.com

Books, PenScore foam, art supplies, and Lutrador:
www.meinketoy.com, www.joggles.com,
www.dickblick.com, www.artquiltingsupplies.com,
www.quiltingarts.com

Discharge paste, textile medium, textile paints,
inkjet fabric sheets, including ExtravOrganza
and Pearl Ex powder:
www.jacquardproducts.com

Fibers for felting:
www.pagewoodfarm.com

Fusible bias tape:
www.nancysnotions.com

Gel and acrylic mediums:
Golden and Liquitex, available at art supply
and crafts stores

Hand-dyed fabrics, organza, and twill tape:
Wendy Richardson, www.qtstudio.com

Hand-dyed fabric bundles:
www.cherrywoodfabrics.com

Paint, photo-transfer paper, soy wax flakes,
prepared-for-dyeing fabrics, textile medium, books,
Pebeo Expandable Paint, Jacquard Discharge Paste,
Jones Tones colored puff paint, Anti-Chlor, dyes and
chemicals, and information online:
www.dharmatrading.com

Painting books, classes, and rubber stamps:
Sherrill Kahn, www.impressmenow.com

Photo-transfer paper:
www.transferartist.com

Print paste SH, dye, Synthrapol, soda ash,
urea, and Pebeo Setacolor paints and medium:
www.prochemicalanddye.com

Printed images:
Ready to Use North American Indian Motifs,
Dover Publications, 1996

Rust-dyeing supplies and instructions:
Lois Jarvis, www.rust-tex.com

Shibori textiles, and ribbons:
email address: glennisd@mac.com

Silk roving:
www.treenwaysilks.com

Stencils, paint sticks, foil for fabric, and foil adhesive:
www.lauramurraydesigns.com

Thermofax screens:
Nancy Mambi, email address:
nancymambi@comcast.net

Threads and Texture Magic shrinking fabric:
www.superiorthreads.com

About the Author

Susan Stein started quilting in 1977 and has delighted in getting other people obsessed with quilting and surface design ever since. A former president and show chairman for Minnesota Quilters, Susan was named Minnesota Quilter of the Year in 2003. She has shared her talents as the author of four books, including *Fabric Art Workshop* and *Fabric Art Projects*, and has contributed to numerous other publications. As a former quilt shop owner and quilting spokesperson, Susan has taught many classes in Minnesota and around the United States. Many of the hundreds of quilts produced by her hands serve as wall hangings, publication pieces, and store samples, while others are on public display or in personal use.

Acknowledgments

Thank you to Shelly Stokes of Cedar Canyon Textiles for her generous donation of paint sticks.

Thank you to Diane Bartels for her numerous donations of art supplies and beautiful fabrics that always fit the bill.

Thank you to all the artists who allowed their beautiful work to be used in this book to illustrate different styles and techniques.

Thank you to all my students who have taught me so much over the years.

And thank you to John for eating late dinners, carrying boxes and boxes of samples that needed to be photographed, fixing my computer, and being a sounding board for ideas.

Index